The Spirit of Freedom: Essays in American History

Edited by Burton W. Folsom, Jr.

The Foundation for Economic Education, Inc.
Irvington-on-Hudson, New York

Cover illustration: Washington Market, New York, 1872. From John Grafton, *New York in the Nineteenth Century,* published by Dover Publications, Inc.

Historical portraits are reproduced from *Dictionary of American Portraits,* edited by Hayward and Blanche Cirker, published by Dover.

Published May 1994
ISBN 0-910614-94-6

Irvington-on-Hudson, NY 10533

Table of Contents

Introduction

One of the great lessons of history is that societies are not naturally free. Most civilizations, from ancient to modern times, have used the power of the state to guide the lives of their citizens—tyrants and priests to direct political life, bureaucrats and guilds to direct economic life. What makes the United States so different is the spirit of freedom that has propelled it from the start. What did we do in our history to create the spirit of freedom, to nurture it in our laws, and to protect it from the advocates of big government? These are questions addressed in *The Spirit of Freedom: Essays in American History*. Each of the essays in this collection touches on the issue of freedom in American history, from the migration of the Pilgrims to the present times.

The Pilgrims provide the classic example of why economic freedom was first tried early in our country's history. Governor William Bradford, in his book *Of Plymouth Plantation,* describes the system of communal agriculture practiced by the Pilgrims in their first two years in the New World. It was, in essence, a socialist experiment: each person produced for the common good and took only what he needed from day to day. Even in such a tight-knit brotherhood of Christians there were apparently some slackers. "The young men, that were most able and fit for labour and service, did repine that they should spend their time and strength to work for other men's wives and children without any recompense," Bradford observed. "The strong, or man of parts, had no more in division of victuals and clothes than he that was weak and not able to do a quarter the other could; this was thought injustice." The result was that the whole colony "languish[ed] in misery."

Governor Bradford and his advisers decided to assign "to every family a parcel of land" and see if they would use their private property to plant more and work harder to bring in the crop. "This had very good success," Bradford recorded, "for it made all hands very industrious. . . . The women now went willingly into the field, and took their little ones with them to set corn; which before would allege weakness and inability. . . ." At the end of the year, the "abler sort" and "more industrious" had plenty "to spare, and sell to others; so as any general want or famine hath not been amongst them since to this day."

The inference from reading Bradford is that the spirit of freedom was created, not imported, in the New World. The American experiment would thus be something new, not a variation on some previous form of despotism. Some 150 years after the Pilgrims introduced a private-property order, Thomas Jefferson wrote the Declaration of Independence and highlighted the spirit of freedom with these words: "We hold these truths to be self-evident, that all men are created equal, that they are endowed by their Creator with certain unalienable rights, that among these are life, liberty, and the pursuit of happiness." The Creator, not the state, is the endower of rights; and the citizens, by implication, are free to keep the fruits of their labor. Furthermore, Jefferson asserted, "to secure these rights, governments are instituted among men, deriving their just powers from the consent of the governed." The Constitution later enshrined this conception of the negative state: the words "no" and "not" are applied to government powers forty-six times in the Constitution and the Bill of Rights. The last sentence of the Bill of Rights reads: "The powers not delegated to the United States by the Constitution; nor prohibited by it to the states, are reserved to the states respectively, or to the people."

During the 1800s, the American experiment with freedom faced two major challenges. First was the expansion of slavery—a problem that took a civil war to resolve. Second was the effort to expand the powers of government beyond those specified in the Constitution. For example, during the 1840s and 1850s, Congress granted $11 million in subsidies to various steamship companies to deliver passengers and mail to and from Europe. During the 1860s and 1870s Congress granted over $60 million in loans and 100 million acres of land to three transcontinental railroads. This type of government involvement in the economy is nowhere mentioned, or even implied, in Article I, section 8 of the Constitution. Furthermore, nonsubsidized entrepreneurs—Cornelius Vanderbilt in steamships and James J. Hill in transcontinentals—clearly outperformed their government-subsidized rivals. Other entrepreneurs flourished in America's relatively free market. John D. Rockefeller led the United States to world dominance in oil; Andrew Carnegie did the same thing in steel. By 1900, the United States had become the world's major industrial power; its freedom and opportunity were attracting almost half a million immigrants each year. Both law and performance, therefore, dictated limited government and individual liberty.

During the 1900s, however, we have seen a rise of big government that has almost quenched the spirit of freedom. The Progressive Era (1900–1920), the New Deal (1930s), and the Great Society (1960s) produced remarkable expansions of government through antitrust laws, railroad regulation, farm subsidies, a Federal Reserve banking system, public works, and massive welfare programs. The obvious question, of course, is why did the United States shift toward more big government and less individual liberty?

Three tentative answers can be put forward. First, in America's strong expanding economy of the late 1800s and early 1900s there were both winners and losers. The losers had incentives to try to use big government to regain their competitive edge. The first two victims of the Sherman Antitrust Act, for example, were James J. Hill and John D. Rockefeller—both dominant figures in railroads and oil. Second, special interests can often achieve their ends much more quickly through political clout rather than through the marketplace. For example, veterans, farmers, and silver miners all lobbied Congress during the New Deal era and received massive government aid for their effort. Third, national crises—wars and depressions, for example—produced cries for government involvement that have permanently increased the role of government in the American economy. Price-fixing, the first federal welfare program, and the FDIC are just three examples of this. Creation of the progressive income tax was central to the expansion of the federal government; Congress enlarged its revenues for new government programs by taxing the rich to give to those special interests that lobby most effectively.

The increase in federal control parallels the decline in individual liberty: entrepreneurs are no longer free to hire whom they want, pay the wages they think are proper, or even produce the products they want. The spirit of freedom is waning. The essays in this volume describe the beginnings of freedom in America, the role of freedom in America's industrial triumph during the 1800s, and the obstacles to freedom posed by big government during the 1900s. They offer important lessons for those who wish to revive that spirit.

—BURTON W. FOLSOM, JR.

I. ORIGINS OF FREEDOM

The Pilgrims in Holland

by Robert A. Peterson

The Dutch have given many things to America: Easter eggs, Santa Claus, waffles, sauerkraut, sleighing, skating, and a host of "vans" and "velts" who helped to build our nation.[1] But perhaps their greatest contribution to America was the 11 years of freedom they gave the Pilgrims—crucial years that helped America's founding fathers work out their philosophy of freedom and prepare for self-government in the New World.

The story of Holland's rise due to free market policies has already been sketched in a previous *Freeman* article.[2] Suffice to say that her struggle for independence from Spain was of epic proportions: when, after a siege of several months, the citizens of Leyden talked of surrender, one burgomaster fortified their spirits by saying, "Here is my sword; plunge it, if you will, into my heart, and divide my flesh among you to appease your hunger; but expect no surrender as long as I am alive."[3] The burgomaster lived—and so did the rest of the citizens of Leyden—to see the day when William the Silent routed the besieging Spaniards. The defense of Leyden turned the tide, and from then on the Dutch never looked back in their fight for freedom. Once they were free, the Dutch embraced much of what we would call a free market philosophy and set up a limited government. In the early 1600s, Holland was the most liberal society in Europe.

It should not surprise us, then, that when English Separatists began to think of emigrating, they thought of Holland. But emigrating to Holland would be no easy task: Englishmen could not leave the country without permission. Never mind—the Separatists would leave secretly. The first group—members of a Brownist church in Gainsborough, went over in 1607; hearing good reports, members of the Scrooby congregation—the group which included many of the Pilgrim

Mr. Peterson is headmaster of The Pilgrim Academy in Egg Harbor City, New Jersey. His articles have appeared in a variety of publications, including *National Review* and *Human Events*. This article is reprinted from the November 1988 issue of *The Freeman*.

Fathers—prepared to follow. After several attempts to escape, the Pilgrims finally succeeded, arriving in Amsterdam on a Dutch ship.

Soon after, they applied to the authorities in Leyden to settle there. John Robinson, their pastor, made a formal application to the Burgomasters and Court of Leyden, stating that about 100 English men and women wanted to come to the city to live "and to have the freedom thereof in carrying on their trades, without being a burden in the least to any one."[4]

The application was granted on February 12, 1609. The Dutch authorities declared that "they refuse no honest persons free ingress to come and have their residence in this city, provided that such persons behave themselves, and submit to the laws and ordinances." Their coming, the Dutch authorities added, "will be agreeable and welcome."[5] As early as the 1600s, the Dutch—with few natural resources of their own—realized the importance of human capital.

The Dutch didn't provide a welcome-wagon of gifts and subsidies: there were no government handouts. What they did offer the Pilgrims was freedom—the freedom to worship according to their consciences as well as to succeed or fail in the Dutch marketplace.

Britain's King James, hearing of the Pilgrims' arrival in Leyden, sent a letter of protest to the town authorities. Jan Van Hout, secretary of the City of Leyden, gave a polite reply, but made no effort either to expel the Pilgrims or to help King James capture them.[6] The Pilgrims were free men.

The Meaning of Freedom

Free men. For the Pilgrims, this was a new idea. Just what did it mean to be free? With the external pressure of persecution lifted, would the Pilgrims remain true to their original calling? Or would they turn liberty into license and lose their distinctive identity? Time would show that the Pilgrims took seriously their responsibilities of self-government. Indeed, the Dutch experience would prove to be an excellent halfway house to the freedom the Pilgrims would find in the New World. For the next 11 years, the Pilgrims took advantage of all the opportunities that Dutch society offered.

Because of their excellent reputation for honesty and hard work, the Pilgrims were able to obtain loans and jobs which they needed to set themselves up in Holland. In a market economy, there is no substi-

John Robinson
(c. 1576–1625)

tute for keeping one's word and honoring contracts. William Bradford, who later became governor of Plymouth Colony, wrote: "And first, though many of them were poor, yet there was none so poor but if they were known to be of that congregation the Dutch (either ba[n]kers or others) would trust them in any reasonable matter when they wanted money, because they found by experience how careful they were to keep their word, and saw them so painful and diligent in their callings. Yea, they would strive to get their custom and to employ them above others in their work, for their honesty and diligence."[7]

Most of the Pilgrims went to work in the textile industry, something for which they had little experience. William Bradford became a fustian worker, while others became weavers, woolcombers, and merchant tailors. In England, almost all had been farmers, following the same patterns of medieval agriculture that their fathers and grandfathers had followed. It must have been hard for grown men to learn a new trade, but it was the price they had to pay to live in a relatively free society. Moreover, it helped to make the Pilgrims an adaptable and teachable people.

At first, the Pilgrims held church services in the homes of various members. But in 1611, the Pilgrims bought a large house to be used for church services and as a residence for their pastor, John Robinson.[8] Left alone by the Dutch, the Pilgrims were finding that Christians could support a church without the aid of government. In Robinson's house, the Pilgrims continued to exercise the congregationalist form of church government which would have such a great impact on American republicanism. The New England town meeting traces its origin to the Congregational church, not to ancient Greece, as many high school history texts erroneously teach.

The Pilgrims also took advantage of Holland's laissez-faire government to set up a small publishing house. Working near the limits of the long arm of King James, William Brewster and Edward Winslow ran a printing press where Puritan tracts and books were published and sent back to England. In all, Brewster published between fifteen and twenty books. Unfortunately, the Dutch could not withstand the pressure from the English government forever, and were compelled to shut down Brewster's press in 1619. Yet they refused to arrest Brewster himself.[9]

Tolerance

The Netherlands' atmosphere of religious freedom tended to have a liberalizing effect on the Pilgrims. John Robinson, for example, was invited to debate at Leyden University. Although he never changed his Separatist views, he did learn that men of different faiths could live together without killing one another. Later, in the New World, Plymouth Colony would prove to be a handy buffer zone between the Puritans' Massachusetts Bay Colony and the more radical colonists in Rhode Island. When Harvard's first president, Henry Dunster, for example, resigned because he came to reject the Puritan doctrine of infant baptism, he settled in Plymouth. The Pilgrims also believed in infant baptism, but they had become tolerant enough to "agree to disagree" with other Christians like Dunster.

The Pilgrims weren't the only ones to benefit from the freedom offered by seventeenth-century Dutch society. Indeed, as one historian put it, there was a steady "flow of exiles, English and Scottish, who sought refuge in Holland from the religious persecution and political violence of seventeenth-century England and Scotland."[10] Literally thousands of English and Scottish Dissenters, unwelcome at Oxford and Cambridge, were educated at the Universities of Leyden and Utrecht. Even John Locke, who had to flee England, benefited from refuge in the Lowlands. Historian Dr. R. Colie has written: "in the city of Amsterdam where writing and printing were so natural to all great minds, Locke began to become Locke, and the obscure political exile turned into the philosopher *par excellence* of a new regime in thought."[11] And when the people of England sought a new pair of monarchs to usher in an age of toleration and freedom, they found them in Holland: William and Mary. The result was England's Glorious Revolution, one of the few bloodless revolutions in history. A year later, England had a Bill of Rights.

The 11 years the Pilgrims spent in Holland saw them grow in responsibility, adaptability, and self-government. As Bradford Smith put it in his biography of William Bradford, "The libertarian tradition at Plymouth, with its profound influence on American life, is not primarily English. It is Dutch. Simple justice demands that we acknowledge this. . . . Thus, during their Leyden years, were the Pilgrims perfecting themselves for the undreamed of work of founding a new nation. In religion, they grew milder and more tolerant. In business and craftsmanship they learned a great deal from the thrifty, ambitious, and highly capable Hollanders. Too, the Dutch flair for efficient government and record-keeping, the spirit of republicanism and civic responsibility were to bear unsuspected fruit in a distant land."[12]

The Pilgrims left Leyden in 1620; William Bradford described their departure in a now-famous passage which later gave the Pilgrims their name: "So they left that goodly and pleasant city which had been their resting place near twelve years; but they knew they were pilgrims, and looked not much on those things, but lift up their eyes to the heavens, their dearest country, and quieted their spirits."[13]

The Mayflower Compact

When the Pilgrims finally landed in America, Separatists and Anglicans joined together to form America's first written constitution—the Mayflower Compact. It was a crucial precedent for self-government in America.

Despite their experience in Holland's free economy, the Pilgrims tried a brief experiment in agricultural socialism when they arrived in America. This experiment, based on a false reading of the Book of Acts, caused widespread starvation. Fortunately, before it was too late, the Pilgrims saw their error and abandoned their "common course" in favor of private property. As Bradford later explained, "This had very good success, for it made all hands very industrious, so as much corn was planted than otherwise would have been by any means the Governor or any other could use, and saved him a great deal of trouble, and gave far better content. . . . The experience that was had in this common course and condition, tried sundry years and that amongst godly and sober men, may well evince the vanity of that conceit of Plato's and other ancients applauded by some of later times; that the taking away of property and bringing in community into a commonwealth would make them happy and flourishing; as if they were wiser than God."[14]

Some present-day historians believe that the Pilgrims have been overrated, that this little band of 100 or so English farmers doesn't deserve such an exalted position in the popular American imagination. Such an attitude is understandable, since most of these same writers disagree with everything for which the Pilgrims stood. Our forefathers knew better. Even before the Revolutionary War, they were celebrating "Old Comers Day" and "Forefathers Day" to honor the coming of the Pilgrims and, more important, the values they represented—including religious, civil, and economic liberty.

This Thanksgiving, let's remember that the material blessings most of us will enjoy this season were made possible by the principles of self-government under God that served the Dutch and the Pilgrims so well in the seventeenth century. Within the space of twenty years, the Pilgrims moved from a static, medieval society to laying the "cornerstone of a nation." We may still profit from their example.

---

1. Thomas A. Bailey and David M. Kennedy, *The American Pageant, Vol. I* (Lexington, Mass.: D. C. Heath and Co., 1979), p. 36.

2. Robert A. Peterson, "Lessons in Liberty: The Dutch Republic, 1579–1750," *The Freeman,* July 1987, pp. 259–264.

3. William Stevenson, *The Story of the Reformation* (Richmond, Va.: John Knox Press, 1959), p. 125.

4. John Brown, *The Pilgrim Fathers of New England and Their Puritan Successor* (New York: Fleming H. Revell, 1896), pp. 120–121.

5. *Ibid.*

6. Mary B. Sherwood, *Pilgrim: A Biography of William Brewster* (Falls Church, Va.: Great Oak Press of Virginia, 1982), p. 117.

7. William Bradford, *Of Plymouth Plantation,* ed. Samuel Eliot Morison (New York: Alfred A. Knopf [1952], 1982), pp. 19–20.

8. Sherwood, p. 123.

9. *Ibid.,* p. 134.

10. Charles Wilson, *The Dutch Republic* (New York: McGraw-Hill Book Co., 1968), p. 183.

11. *Ibid.,* p. 175.

12. Bradford Smith, *Bradford of Plymouth* (Philadelphia: Lippincott, 1951), p. 78.

13. Bradford, p. 47.

14. *Ibid.,* pp. 120–121.

The Puritan Experiment in Common Ownership

by Gary North

One of the more familiar incidents in American history, at least within conservative circles, is the disastrous experiment with a common storehouse in the Pilgrim colony in 1621–1623. Governor Bradford describes in some detail in his history of the colony how young men refused to work in the common fields in order to lay up produce for a common storehouse, only to see all goods divided equally among families. Upon petition of the planters, the Governor and his council decided to follow their advice: assign families their personal plots of farm land (according to family size) and abolish the common storehouse. Immediately, men and women returned to the harvest fields.

What is less known about this incident is how the little colony ever made such a disastrous decision in the first place. The fact of the matter is that the colonists had never wanted to inaugurate a system of totally common property. The group of British "adventurers" that had supplied the Pilgrim exiles in Holland with traveling money and capital had insisted that the colony be made a part of the joint-stock company. The assets of the colony therefore were the assets of the company, headquartered in Britain, and the agricultural products were to be shared equally among company members, both colonial and British. Governor Bradford was the chief agent of the company in New England; hence, he was compelled to impose the common storehouse system.

In the original negotiations it had been understood that profits would be shared by all members of the company, but the colonists had not agreed to the sharing of houses, gardens, and other improved land. They were informed of these terms only as they were about to leave for North America, and as they left, they sent back word to the merchant adventurers that their agents who had agreed to such terms had not been empowered to do so.[1] But the continuing dependence upon

---

Dr. North, is president of the Institute for Christian Economics, Tyler, Texas. This article, which appeared in the April 1974 issue of *The Freeman,* is reprinted with the permission of the author.

the company for resources during the first year of the colony's existence compelled them to give in to the company's terms.[2]

The story did not end in 1623, when necessity forced the hands of the colonists. In 1627, the bickering British directors sold out their interests in the colony to the settlers for £1,800. The settlers were to spend a decade and a half in paying off their debt, and at times had to borrow extra time at rates of 30 percent to 50 percent. Nevertheless, they persisted and finally repaid the debt, in 1642.

In 1627, shortly after buying out the British directors, Governor Bradford supervised the division of the colony's assets among the settlers. First, they divided livestock. There were few animals, so the 156 people (less than four families) were divided into a dozen companies; each company received a cow and two goats. In January of 1628, the land was divided, this time by random lot. Complaints about unequal housing were forestalled by requiring those who received better housing to make an equalizing payment to those receiving poorer housing. Peace was preserved.

There was one decision, however, which was to prove costly. Meadow was in short supply, so it was kept in common ownership. Furthermore, fishing, fowling, and water remained "open" to all settlers.[3] The Pilgrims were to have the same difficulties with the administration of these common fields as their neighbors, the Puritans, were to experience. Only after 1675, when the "commons" throughout New England were increasingly distributed to the families in each town, were these problems overcome.

Varying Concepts of Ownership

In order to understand the thinking of the first half century of New England settlers, we have to realize that these immigrants did not bring over from England some universally accepted concept of land ownership. There was an obvious tendency for groups of settlers from one region in England to establish homogeneous townships in Massachusetts. English towns had developed at least three major systems of land tenure: the open-field system, the closed-field system, and the incorporated borough. All three appeared in New England in the early years.

The open-field system stressed the community administration of land. It is this system which we generally associate with the word "medieval," although the Middle Ages saw many systems of land tenure. Sumner Chilton Powell has described these systems in some detail in his fine study, *Puritan Village*. The open-field system "regarded the advantages of the area as communal property, to be shared by all. No one was to exclude a neighbor from such a necessity as good meadow, or the down, or the woods. And if anyone practiced such exclusion, or attempted to increase the amount of his holding at the expense of his neighbors, all villagers reacted instantly to restore their 'rights.'"[4] Needless to say, this approach did not survive long in the setting of New England.

Extensive Trading of Land in Berkhamsted

Quite different was an English borough like Berkhamsted. In the early seventeenth century, over one thousand acres "were opened up, bought, or traded, in countless individual transactions. If the men of Berkhamsted were doing nothing else, they were trading land."[5] The legend of the Yankee trader was rooted in this sort of English inheritance. There were some enclosed lands, but most of the farmers were shifting as rapidly as possible to a system of individual farm management.

A third system was a sort of combination, the closed-field system of East Anglia. "There was one common pasture, but each farmer was expected to provide a balance of arable, pasture, and hay meadow for himself. He succeeded, or failed on his own farming ability."[6] One of the problems in a Massachusetts town like Sudbury was the diversity of backgrounds of its inhabitants. There was no agreement as to where the locus of economic sovereignty should be. Should it be the individual farmer? Should it be the town's selectmen who controlled the resources of the town commons?

The towns and colonial governments of seventeenth-century New England were not strictly theocracies; ordained ministers could not be elected to political office. But they were important as advisers. Furthermore, the laymen of that era were very often more theologically motivated than ministers of this century. Most of the towns were regarded as tightly knit Christian commonwealths by their inhabitants, and during the first fifty years of their existence, they imposed restrictions on immigration into the local community. They were concerned that newcomers might not meet the religious and moral standards of the present inhabitants. As late as 1678, the records of Plymouth Colony offered the hope that "the Court will be careful, that whom they accept are persons orthodox in their judgments." The Puritan towns of Boston, Cambridge, Dedham, and probably many others all included the requirement that outsiders be cleared by town officials before they were allowed to buy land locally. Braintree even included a restriction on land sales (though not explicitly religious in intent) that local residents would have the right to bid first on all property offered for sale to outsiders.

It is significant that in the final quarter of the century, these religious restrictions were generally dropped. Instead, a new requirement—in fact, a new emphasis on an old requirement—appeared: restrictions on immigrants who might become a burden on the welfare rolls. The towns had steadily become more pluralistic theologically, but the fear of an increase in tax rates was a truly ecumenical device. By offering economic support to local indigents, the townspeople were afraid that outsiders might take advantage of this legal charity. Barriers to entry followed in the wake of "free" goods, however modest—and they were very modest—the size of the public welfare allotments.[7]

Pressure on the Commons

The fear of increased welfare burdens was not the only economic issue confronting established communities every time a stranger sought admission as a resident of some town. In the early years of settlement, each town had considerable land—six to eight miles square—and relatively few inhabitants. Each resident had legal access to the common pasturage and to any future divisions of land from the huge blocs owned by the town. But as the number of inhabitants increased, and as more and more distributions of town land reduced the available source of unowned land, the per capita supply of land began to shrink. Those inhabitants who had a share in the common pasture and the common lands sought to protect their control over further use and distributions of such property. In town after town, a new rule was imposed: outsiders had to purchase access to rights in the common property from local inhabitants. The result was a new appreciation of private ownership and private control of property, even among men who had grown up in English communities that had used the open-field system of farming. The land hunger of New England after 1650 created new incentives to gain and exercise personal sovereignty over the chief economic resource, land.

There was another incentive to reduce the size of the community-owned property: bureaucratic wrangling. Page after page of the Massachusetts town records, year after year: how to restrain access to the common meadow? How to keep midnight visitors from cutting down choice trees for firewood or other uses? How to keep the meadow's fences in repair? Statute followed statute, to no avail. Fines were imposed, equally to no avail. "Free" land meant strong demand for its productivity, and town leaders never were able to find a rational, efficient means of restricting uneconomic uses of the town property. Men had a strong incentive to further their personal economic ends, and far less incentive to consider the public's position. The commons served as incentives to waste, for without a free market and private ownership, it was impossible to calculate accurately the costs and benefits associated with the use of the land. This is the chief economic flaw of all socialist systems, and the early settlers of New England were unable to solve it.

The Eternal Problems of Supply and Demand

Someone who has only a superficial knowledge of the history of the Puritans of the Massachusetts Bay Colony tends to see them as men obsessed with imposing religious restraints or moral restraints on private activities. They were concerned with such questions, as the records indicate, but from the bulk of the legislation, two problems were eternal, unsolvable, and endlessly bothersome to Puritan leaders: pigs without rings in their noses running through the town, and midnight tree-cutters on the commons. The tree-cutters, like the pigs, insisted on sticking their noses into other people's property.

The commoners—those who had legal access to the common fields and meadows—were too often involved in what today is known as "free riding." They planted crops in the common property, but neglected to keep their portion of the commons properly fenced. It was almost impossible to keep track of who was responsible for which plot. Towns had to intervene and assign plots, thus creating opportunities for local political dissension. Animals that wandered around the fenced land often broke down unrepaired fencing between plots, getting into someone else's crops. Tension here was continual.

Fencing inspectors were important officials in every town. Conflicts over responsibility were endless. Without private plots privately repaired, such conflicts were inevitable. In the early decades of Massachusetts, no single public policy prevailed long. First, the colony's General Court—the chief legislative agency—placed the responsibility for fencing on the local town; then it placed the responsibility on the local individual citizen; next it switched back to its original position of town control. The statutes did not function well in practice. Different communities had different problems, and the central government had difficulty in dealing with all of them through the use of any single administrative policy.[8]

The problem facing every selectman in every New England village was "the tragedy of the commons," as the biologist Garrett Hardin has called it. Each person who has access to the benefits of public property for use in his own personal business has a positive incentive to drain additional resources from the commons, and he has a very low or even negative incentive to restrain him. The costs of his actions are borne by all the "owners," while the benefits are strictly individual. One more cow or sheep or goat grazing on the town commons will register no noticeable increase in the communally assessed economic burden which rests on any single individual. Yet such grazing is immediately beneficial to the owner of the animal. High benefits, low costs: "Each man is locked into a system that compels him to increase his herd without limit—in a world that is limited."[9] It is not surprising that selectmen would find themselves burdened with endless disputes concerning the size of the local herds and the proper—"fair"—assessments of the economic costs of running those herds on the commons.

There is an answer to the tragedy of the commons, at least where it is inexpensive to assign property rights. As C. R. Batten has argued, the transfer of ownership from an amorphous common group to individual citizens provides an incentive to reduce the demands made on the land. Private owners have to assess both costs and benefits of any activity, seeing to it that costs do not outrun benefits. By the end of the seventeenth century, Puritan leaders—or at least leaders who were the descendants of Puritans—reached a similar conclusion.[10]

With each piece of legislation, another problem or set of problems appeared. First, only actual town commoners could run their animals in the common meadow or in the outlying common lands. Only local residents could cut the trees. Later, the selectmen had to impose limits on the number of cattle that could be run, frequently on a "one cow per man" rule. Each man was assessed a few shillings per year for this right. Some people brought in horses; Boston banned them on Sundays. Sheep had to be supervised by a sheepherder. As more animals required full-time supervision, towns hired herdsmen. To keep the cost per beast low, each town resident was required by law to run his animal with the herd. Cambridge, for example, imposed a fine of one shilling on anyone whose cow was found on his land after 8 a.m. Since the driver left at 6 a.m., anyone who had not yet delivered his animal to the herd had to escort his cow to the driver, eating up scarce time. A similar law for goats was passed two years later, in 1639.[11] People naturally attempted to evade the law, and by 1648 the revenues supporting the town's herdsman were not meeting his salary. Consequently, in typical interventionist fashion, the selectmen decided to assess all men a certain amount, whether or not they ran cattle on the commons.[12] A similar rule was established in Watertown in 1665, and the massive evasions encouraged the selectmen to pass an even stiffer law in 1670.[13]

Corrected Over Time

The confusion reigned for decades. As the Watertown records report so eloquently, "there being many complaints made concerning the disorderliness of cattle and swine and the multitudes of sheep in the town, it was voted that the matter above mentioned is left with the selectmen to consider something that may tend to reformation and to present what they shall do to the town to be confirmed."[14] Needless to say, the selectmen could not do anything about it, any more than half a century of Puritan town governments before them. The only solution was the distribution of the commons to local inhabitants—the demise of the commons.

Traditional patterns of life do not die out overnight. Men are usually unwilling to change their way of life unless forced to do so, either by economic circumstances or by direct political pressure. The little town of Sudbury was a case in question. Its inhabitants clung to the old English system of communal property management. The access to the commons was restricted, in 1655, and at least thirty younger men received no meadow grants for their animals. They went out of the selectmen's meeting ready to fight. Fight they did, until the town was split. They formed a new community down the road, Marlborough. Not gaining access to the local commons, they were perfectly willing to settle for a 24,000-acre plot a few miles away.[15]

Factional strife was not a part of the original goals of the founders of New England. Factionalism was a blight to be avoided; this opinion remained a touchstone of American political thought until James Madison wrote Federalist #10. Yet the quarreling over the commons was incessant, in direct opposition to the political and communal ideal of the peaceable kingdom.

"Togetherness"

The town of Sudbury was not to be the only Puritan village unable to cope successfully with centrifugal forces created by the presence of socialized property within the town limits. The creation of Marlborough, despite the fact that the young founders also established a town commons, testified to the difficulty of preserving both the old common field tenure system and social peace in the midst of vast stretches of unoccupied land. It was too easy to move out, and this feature of New England was to erode the medievalism of early Puritan thought. The centralized social control necessary to enforce such a system of common land required the existence of widespread land scarcity. Ironically, it was in the final quarter of the seventeenth century that such land scarcity appeared—scarcity of the most productive lands—but by that time the haggling over the administration of the commons and increasing land values had already provided the incentives necessary to convince both leaders and average citizens that the commons should be distributed permanently.

One of the original goals of the founders of New England was that of social cohesion. The life of each community was to be religiously based. The church was the center of the town, both symbolically and very often physically. Men were to live close to one another, share in one another's burdens, pray together, and construct God's kingdom on earth. But there was a strong economic incentive to consolidate landholdings.

Even before the market of Boston created demand for agricultural products, men in the villages had begun to barter their land allotments. A man might live in the town with five or six acres of garden and meadow, and he might also have been given some forty- or fifty-acre plots in the common lands scattered around the town. Obviously, it was to the advantage of some men to consolidate their holdings, trading with others who also wanted to cut down on the time spent to travel—in mud, in snow, in dust—from one plot to another. Then, family by family, an exodus began from the central town. Artisans tended to come into the town's center; farmers, especially those affected by Boston's market (those in the immediate Boston area or close to water transport to Boston), needed to consolidate in order to rationalize production.

Despite the efforts of ministers and local selectmen, the population spread out; decentralization, when not political, was at least social. You could not examine your neighbor's intimate affairs when he was three miles away. The market for land was an agent of social decentralization.

The Urge for Privacy

The experience of the isolated little town of Dedham is illustrative of the effect of market freedom on traditional patterns of social and economic control. Professor Kenneth Lockridge describes the process:

> If the corporate unity of the village was slowly eroding, so was its physical coherence. The common-field system began disintegrating almost from the day of its inception. Already in the 1640's the town permitted men to "fence their lots in particular" and presumably to grow in these lots whichever crops they wished. By the 1670's it had become usual for men to take up both special "convenience grants" and their usual shares of each new dividend in locations as close as possible to their existing lots, practices which aided the consolidation of individual holdings. The process encouraged by public policy was completed by private transactions, for an active market in small parcels soon emerged, a market in which most farmers sought to sell distant lands and buy lands closer to their main holdings. The net result was the coalescence of private farms. From here, it would be but two short steps for farmers whose

> holdings were centered in outlying areas to move their barns and then their houses from the village out to their lands. As of 1686 few seem to have taken these steps, but the way had been prepared and the days of a society totally enclosed by the village were numbered. In any event the common-field system was gone, taking with it the common decisions and the frequent encounters of every farmer with his fellows which it entailed.[16]

The closer to Boston, the faster these changes occurred, for if transport was cheap enough—within ten miles or so along a well-traveled road—the effects of the free market were felt far more alluringly. It paid to become more efficient.

A Typical Development

The demise of the commons in Cambridge seems typical. The first division took place in 1662. A second followed in 1665. Two small divisions were made in 1707 and 1724. Various methods were used to determine who got what parcels of land: lots were drawn, or acres were distributed in terms of the number of cows a family was allowed to graze on the common meadow, or a committee was formed to consider other methods. In some towns there was considerable strife; in others, the distributions were relatively peaceful. The effects on Cambridge were significant, and in retrospect they seem quite predictable. After 1691 it was no longer necessary to pass new laws against the cutting of timber from the commons. Men owned their own land, and they cut or refused to cut as they saw fit. It was no longer necessary to pass laws against selling timber to men from other towns, a common feature of mid-seventeenth-century legislation in the towns. A thoroughly individualistic system of land tenure evolved.

The final impetus to private ownership came in the 1680s. James II, after coming to the throne in 1685, sent Sir Edmund Andros, the former Royal governor of New York, to take over as governor general of New England. The king meant to consolidate the political structure of the colonies, making them all purely royal colonies. Andros met with instant opposition. He began to hit too close to a crucial legal weakness of New England's towns.

By 1685, there were four New England colonies, New Haven

having been absorbed into Connecticut in 1662: Massachusetts, Plymouth, Connecticut, and Rhode Island. (Plymouth became a part of Massachusetts in 1692.) The right of these colonial governments to create valid, legal townships was in question; the right of the towns to act as if they were incorporated entities in giving legal title to land was not in doubt: it was illegal. The king's seal was not present in the towns, and this was an invitation for the king's newly appointed bureaucracy—a growing horde—to intervene to their own advantage.

In 1686, the Andros regime imposed a 2.5 shilling quit-rent per annum on all 100-acre lots not occupied or occupied by means of defective titles. Andros called for a re-examination of the land patents. Whether or not this represented a true threat to the majority of land owners, they certainly were convinced that his intentions were the worst, and that a major land-grab was about to be inaugurated. In the various political pamphlets issued in 1688–90 by outraged critics of his administration (later assembled as the *Andros Tracts*), this criticism was made over and over. It was a major reason cited as a justification for his overthrow in 1688. "Henceforward, the colonies took absolute control of the land."[17] Men desired, as never before, to gain clear-cut title to their lands. It intensified a pressure that was five decades old or more.[18]

The Market Process

Step by step, individual men asserted their sovereignty over land; the proprietors of the commons steadily transferred the unoccupied land surrounding the village, as well as the land in the more central common fields, to the citizens of the town. While they did not ask for competitive bidding as a means of distributing this land, the officials did effect a continuous transformation of ownership. In doing so, they established a break from the historical inheritance of many towns, the old medieval open-field system of common ownership. The continual bickering over the allocation of timber, fallen logs, tree cutting by moonlight, town herds, herdsmen's salaries, fence mending, planting in the common fields, and policing everyone to see that these laws were obeyed, finally broke the will of the town officials. It was easier to give the land away; it was also more profitable for town residents, in most cases.

The tradition of the independent yeoman farmer so impressed

Jefferson that he built an entire political philosophy around it. The idea that individual men are more responsible for the administration of property than boards of political appointees or even elected officials became a fundamental principle of eighteenth- and nineteenth-century American life. The concepts of personal responsibility and personal authority became interlocked, and the great symbol of this fusion was the family farm. The endless quest for land by American families is one of the most impressive tales in American history. It began as soon as the Pilgrims stepped off the *Mayflower* and their Puritan neighbors stepped off the *Arabella* a decade later. The experiment in common ownership in village after village over half a century convinced ministers, laymen, and political leaders that the private ownership of the means of production was not only the most efficient way to get Christian goals accomplished, but also that such a form of ownership was economically profitable as well. They saw, almost from the start, that social peace is best achieved by means of the private ownership of the tools of production, especially that most crucial of tools, land. The lessons of that first half-century of New England Puritan life is one of the most important heritages of American life. Without it, indeed, American life would be impossible to interpret correctly.

---

1. George D. Langdon, Jr.; *Pilgrim Colony* (New Haven: Yale University Press, 1966), p. 9.
2. *Ibid.,* p. 26.
3. *Ibid.,* p. 31.
4. Sumner Chilton Powell, *Puritan Village* (Garden City, N.Y.: Doubleday Anchor [1963] 1966), p. 11.
5. *Ibid.,* p. 26.
6. *Ibid.,* p. 72.
7. On the size of local town charities, see Stephen Foster, *Their Solitary Way: The Puritan Social Ethic in the First Century of Settlement in New England* (New Haven: Yale University Press, 1971), p. 137.
8. William B. Weeden, *Economic and Social History of New England, 1620–1789* (2 vols., 1890), I, pp. 59–60.
9. Garrett Hardin, "The Tragedy of the Commons," *Science* (December 13, 1968); reprinted in Garrett de Bell (ed.), *The Environmental Handbook* (New York: Ballantine, 1970), p. 37.
10. C. R. Batten, "The Tragedy of the Commons," *The Freeman,* October 1970.
11. *The Records of the Town of Cambridge, Massachusetts, 1630–1703* (1901), pp. 28, 39.
12. *Ibid.,* p. 72.
13. *Watertown Records* (1894), I, pp. 92, 94–95.
14. *Ibid.,* p. 142.
15. Powell, *Puritan Village,* chapter 9.
16. Kenneth Lockridge, *A New England Town* (New York: Norton, 1970), p. 82.

17. Roy H. Akagi, *The Town Proprietors of the New England Colonies* (Gloucester, Mass.: Peter Smith [1924] 1963), p. 124.

18. Philip J. Greven, *Four Generations: Population, Land, and Family in Colonial Andover, Massachusetts* (Ithaca, N. Y.: Cornell University Press, 1970), p. 61.

Holy Experiment

by Paul Luther Brindle

The Holy Experiment was the name given by William Penn to his colonization on the west bank of the Delaware River. William Penn was sure that he was directed by God through his Inner Light. When he was 12 years old, and alone in his room, he had a spiritual experience which he described as God appearing unto him and making it clear to him that there was important work for him to perform.

William Penn was born October 14, 1644, almost within the shadow of the Tower of London. His father was an English Navy Captain whose name was also William. His mother was Dutch, the former Margaret Jasper, and is credited with giving him his unshakeable poise. The father had been taught the way of the sea by his father, Giles Penn, on his own ship in the sailing-vessel days and in the rough-and-tumble merchant service. Sir William Penn became Vice Admiral and was knighted. As recipient of many honors, he was invited to state functions, where he felt humbled by his limited formal education. He determined that his son should be educated as a courtier.

A tutor was engaged and young William was sent to Chigwell School in Essex, then to Oxford University for two years, and then to Soumur in France where he lived with, and was influenced by, the noted Calvinist theologian Moses Amyrault, a man of learning and eloquence.

Penn wore fine clothes, armor, and side-arms becoming the cavalier gentry, and young men of distinction. While at Oxford, Penn had developed skills in fencing, and when an attacker in Paris drew his sword because of some imaginary offense, Penn bested him. Penn could have pierced through, but he turned his attacker free unharmed. Penn, by now the theologian, said concerning the incident, "I know no religion which destroys courtesy, civility and kindness." This led him to give up armor and side-arms.

Mr. Brindle, a Washington, D.C., attorney, wrote this article for the February 1975 issue of *The Freeman*. His paternal ancestors arrived in Philadelphia in 1715, from Liverpool.

William Penn
(1644–1718)

Penn went to the London Inn to study English law until his father took him to his estate in Ireland to avoid the plague of 1665 and 1666.

In Ireland, Penn heard the Quaker Thomas Loe, who preached, "There is a faith that overcomes the world and a faith that the world overcomes," and from that time Penn was a steadfast member of the Society of Friends. The Quakers were delighted to secure a convert from the Cavalier class, a man of family, education, wealth, and prominence. He became a recognized Quaker leader, preacher, and author of numerous theological works.

Seventeenth-century life in England was at a low ebb, with 250 crimes punishable by death—usually on the block. The Conventicle Act of 1664 made it unlawful to hold any religious meeting other than that of the authorized Church of England. Magistrates were allowed to impose fines upon violation, often amounting to confiscation of assets and imprisonment without trial by jury. The informer's fee was one-third of the fine. The Quakers refused to obey the Conventicle

Act, and worshiped openly as Quakers. As a result, men, women, and children were arrested and carted off to prison, and the following week there would be replacements to suffer the same fate.

A Quaker in Prison

Newgate Prison was overcrowded. While in prison there, Penn spent most of his time writing *The Great Case of Liberty of Conscience* and on another occasion he wrote, *No Cross, No Crown,* which has been reprinted from time to time.

Later, Penn spent eight months and 16 days in the Tower of London without trial. Word reached him that the Bishop of London had vowed to keep him there until he died. To this Penn replied, "They are mistaken in me, I value not their threats; I will weary out their malice."

During Penn's incarceration in the Tower, he was without research material, but his writings included accurate quotations and analyses of the opinions of over 150 personages of the past and present. When the book, *Innocency with Her Open Face,* was published and reached the streets, it was so helpful in authenticating his claim of his Inner Light, as a man of God, and stirred such a clamor, that in a few days he was released from prison by the act of pardon.

Property Seized, Later Restored

Large numbers of Quakers were refusing to pay tithes, or taxes to maintain the government, which included support of the established church. The sheriff was obliged to seize their property and sell it to obtain treble the amount of the tax, or to imprison them.

The Quakers refused to take an oath, or to remove their hats in court, church, or in the presence of important persons. They denied the validity of all sacraments, including baptism and the Lord's Supper. They declared that a man should not be bound to believe more than his reason could comprehend. The Quakers were attempting to harken back to first-century Christianity, and thereby circumvent 16 centuries of growth and struggle of Christendom. Their position on primitive Christianity was to become an important point of understanding with the Indians in America.

The Test Act of 1673 barred from public office (both civil and military) all who refused the sacrament according to the rites of the Church of England. This forced the resignation of James Stuart, the Duke of York, from his position of Lord High Admiral of the Navy. James was openly a Romanist, while Charles II was secretly of the same faith.

Ten years after the death of Admiral Sir William Penn, Charles II was still unable to pay the estate the Admiral's uncollected salary and loans which amounted to about £16,000. William Penn was at the peak of his influence. He proposed that the Crown convey to him the uncolonized land west of the Delaware River in North America in exchange for the indebtedness and, at the same time, to provide a haven for the religiously oppressed in England. It had been sixty years since the Pilgrims had settled in Massachusetts for the free worship of the Puritan religion, and Penn saw a need for individual religious liberty.

When the Charter for the grant was being considered in Council, on March 4, 1681, Penn stood with his hat on, as was the custom, although he was in presence of the King. When the King removed his hat, Penn asked, "Friend Charles, why dost thou not keep on thy hat?" His Majesty replied laughingly, "It is the custom in this place for only one person to remain covered at one time."

Penn, in deference to the Quaker restriction against vanity, objected to the colony being named Pennsylvania, the Latin for Penn's woods. In response the King said, "I will name it after your father." On March 4, 1681, the Holy Experiment was launched, and March 4 was later selected as the Inauguration of the Presidents of the United States—a custom which prevailed through 1933.

Pennsylvania became a proprietorship colony in America. It consisted of 45,000 square miles, only 5,000 square miles less than the area of England. Of it Penn wrote, "'Tis a clear and just thing; and my God, which has given it to me, through many difficulties, will I believe, bless and make it the seed of a nation. I shall tender care to the government that it may be well laid at first."

Address to Settlers

Penn lost no time in putting the Holy Experiment into effect, as inspired by his Inner Light. On April 8, 1681, he wrote to the settlers in Pennsylvania—the Swedes, Dutch, and English—in a style which has sometimes been referred to as Governor Penn's Inaugural Address. He wrote, in part:

> My Friends:
>
> I wish you all happiness, here and hereafter. I have to let you know that it has pleased God in his Providence to cast you within my lot and care. It is a business that, though I never undertook before, yet God has given me an understanding of my duty, and an honest mind to do it uprightly, I hope you will not be troubled with your change and the king's choice, for you are now fixt, at the mercy of no Governour that comes to make his fortune great; you shall be governed by laws of your own making, and live a free, and, if you will, a sober and industrious people. I shall not usurp the right of any, or oppress his person; God has furnished me with a better resolution, and has given me the grace to keep it. In short, whatever sober and free men can reasonably desire for the security and improvement of their own happiness, I shall heartily comply with.... I beseech God to direct you in the way of righteousness, and therein prosper you and your children after you. I am,
>
> Your true friend,
> Wm. Penn.

When Penn first arrived in his colony on October 27, 1682, at Uplands (renamed Chester), he immediately began to apply his frame of government. He issued writs for the election of Representatives to the assembly to meet at Chester on December 4, 1682. Penn was delighted to find the great storehouse of riches which exceeded his fondest expectations. Prior to going to Pennsylvania, he had written several letters to the Lenni Lenape (Delaware) Indians, which had been read and translated to them. The letters were friendly and deeply religious, and he assured them that his people would never harm them nor take their land without payment.

He learned their language and would walk among them. The Indians had strong likes and dislikes, but were deeply fond of Penn, whose brotherly love was contagious. The Indians shared Penn's convictions on immortality. Penn contended, "That the truest end in life is to know the life that never ends—that death is no more than turning us over from time to eternity."

After making land purchases in 1683, Penn wrote: "The poor people are under a dark night in things relating to religion, to be sure, the tradition of it, yet they believe in God and Immortality, without the help of metaphysicks; for they say, there is a great king that made them, who dwells in a glorious country to the southward of them, and that the souls of the good shall go thither where they shall live again."

Penn's Fundamental Constitutions of Government read: "That all persons living in the province who confess and acknowledge the Almighty and Eternal God to be Creator, Upholder and Ruler of the world—subject to the general rules of piety, all were welcome. Only those who denied the existence of God should be excluded."

The Frame of Government

Penn looked upon the state as evil and wanted no more government than the ill-behaved of worldly citizens made necessary. His philosophy of an ideal society was one in which men governed themselves and their affairs so well and justly that formal government would have little or nothing to do. Penn said, "Liberty without obedience is confusion and obedience without liberty is slavery." Imprisonments were continuing in England, requiring courtier attention. Penn sailed on August 16, 1684, to England.

King Charles II died in 1685, and his younger brother James Stuart ascended to the throne as James II, and declared that he would establish the Roman religion in England or die in the attempt. Charles had a natural son, Monmouth, for whom a Dukedom had been created. He mustered his forces to take the throne from his uncle, James II, which resulted in a bloody failure, and Monmouth lost his head on the block. It took William of Orange with 14,000 well-disciplined Dutch troops to rout his father-in-law from the throne. James tossed the great seal into the Thames and fled to France where he lived on the bounty of Louis XIV. This was the end of Penn's influence as a courtier.

At the behest of William in 1689, eight years after Penn's Holy Experiment began, Parliament passed the Toleration Act, which William had promised when he announced his intention to drive James from the throne. The Act established religious liberty by law. The reforms established were the very ones for which Penn, in his earlier days, had so ardently contended, and modern England was to grow up under these reforms.

William and Mary

Under the reign of William and Mary, violence, cruelty, and brutal executions largely passed away. Mary was the daughter of James II and his first wife, Anne Hyde, and was reared as a Protestant. She and William were virtuous and honorable monarchs, and set an example for all rulers to follow. The statesman who failed lost his office, not his head. Under the liberties established by William III, the modern world was beginning to appear. The Toleration Act brought tranquility to the English people, and cleared the way for dealing with those of different religions and cultures.

Penn visited Holland and Germany, preaching to the oppressed Mennonites and Schwenkfelders, and urged them to colonize in Pennsylvania. He visited Princess Elizabeth, granddaughter of James I, who was then the Abbess of Hereford, and who entertained an interest in the mysteries of the Deity. Penn, accompanied by Quaker missionaries, was hopeful of her acceptance of Quakerism. Wrote Penn in his notes: "The gospel was preached, the dead . . . raised and the living were comforted."

In 1699 Penn made his second trip to Pennsylvania, when the population was about 20,000, consisting of about one-third members of the Church of England, one-third Quakers, and one-third Presbyterians, Mennonites, and others. When Penn, a man of great poise, visited throughout the province and the neighboring colonies of New York, New Jersey, and Maryland, he was graciously received.

Penn returned to England in 1701, but before his departure, a new and simpler constitution was adopted by the people. Penn stoutly maintained that there should be:

1. no establishment of the Church of England as the state church;
2. no use of public funds for sectarian benefit;
3. no abridgment of suffrage;
4. no Test Act eligibility for office; and
5. no direct parliamentary taxation upon property or income.

In compliance with Leviticus 25:10, a huge bell was cast by Pass and Stow of Philadelphia, and was rung on the fiftieth Anniversary, proclaiming liberty throughout the land. It was again rung in jubilation on July 4, 1776, and each year thereafter until a crack developed. After that, it became an attraction for visitors.

Those whom Penn left in charge of his province were soon to be operating it at a loss, and Penn was imprisoned for debt. To terminate the loss in his advancing years, he offered a sacrifice sale of Pennsylvania to the Crown, for £12,000, and accepted £1,200 as advance payment.

When the new constitution was adopted in 1701, the first of the prohibitions (against a state church) was inadvertently omitted, and Penn by recoupment, tried to incorporate it as a restrictive covenant in the sales agreement, but destiny had another plan for the survival of the Holy Experiment.

Penn suffered a stroke which rendered him unable to contract during his remaining years. It fell to the lot of his widow, Hannah, to save the Holy Experiment. She ended the foolish sales talks, repaid the advance from an inheritance, schooled herself in the affairs of the province, and taught the same to her sons.

The Order of Succession in Pennsylvania

Thomas Penn was the businessman of the family. Later he became Governor and he instructed his nephew, John Penn, to succeed him. John Penn served until the Revolution.

Written high in the capitol at Harrisburg are William Penn's famous words, "The nations want an example and my God will give them one." By liberating the spirits of men, more power was released through the Holy Experiment than was theretofore thought possible by those of lesser stature.

The Quakers opposed war per se, and even as a means of defense. They surrendered political power as early as 1757. During and after the Revolution, many Quakers emigrated to Canada.

Penn had placed happiness foremost in his letter to the settlers in 1681, and 95 years later when Philadelphia was the most populous city in America, it was paraphrased as the "pursuit of happiness" in the Declaration of Independence. Seven of the 39 signers to the Declaration of Independence were Pennsylvanians, and Pennsylvania was the first of the larger states to ratify the U.S. Constitution, on December 12, 1787, following only five days after ratification by Delaware, a land formerly owned by Penn and settled as a part of the Holy Experiment.

The Holy Experiment in representative government, by strange circumstances, remained not the work of any one person, or group of persons. Succeeding generations and freedom-loving immigrants could find inspiration from Penn's dedicatory prayer inscribed on Philadelphia's City Hall, the closing words of which are, "To preserve thee from such as would abuse and defile thee that thou mayest be preserved to the end."

A Tale of Two Revolutions

by Robert A. Peterson

The year 1989 marks the 200th anniversary of the French Revolution. To celebrate, the French government is throwing its biggest party in at least 100 years, to last all year. In the United States, an American Committee on the French Revolution has been set up to coordinate programs on this side of the Atlantic, emphasizing the theme "France and America: Partners in Liberty."

But were the French and American Revolutions really similar? On the surface, there were parallels. Yet over the past two centuries, many observers have likened the American Revolution to the bloodless Glorious Revolution of 1688, while the French Revolution has been considered the forerunner of the many modern violent revolutions that have ended in totalitarianism. As the Russian naturalist, author, and soldier Prince Piotr Kropotkin put it, "What we learn from the study of the Great [French] Revolution is that it was the source of all the present communist, anarchist, and socialist conceptions."[1]

It is because the French Revolution ended so violently that many Frenchmen are troubled about celebrating its 200th anniversary. French author Leon Daudet has written: "Commemorate the French Revolution? That's like celebrating the day you got scarlet fever." An anti-'89 movement has even begun to sell mementos reminding today's Frenchmen of the excesses of the Revolution, including Royalist black armbands and calendars that mock the sacred dates of the French Revolution.

The French should indeed be uneasy about their Revolution, for whereas the American Revolution brought forth a relatively free economy and limited government, the French Revolution brought forth first anarchy, then dictatorship.

Eighteenth-century France was the largest and most populous country in western Europe. Blessed with rich soil, natural resources, and a long and varied coastline, France was Europe's greatest power

---

Mr. Peterson is headmaster of The Pilgrim Academy in Egg Harbor City, New Jersey.
This article was originally published in the August 1989 issue of *The Freeman*.

and the dominant culture on the continent. Unfortunately, like all the other countries of eighteenth-century Europe, France was saddled with the economic philosophy of mercantilism. By discouraging free trade with other countries, mercantilism kept the economies of the European nation-states in the doldrums, and their people in poverty.

Nevertheless, in 1774, King Louis XVI made a decision that could have prevented the French Revolution by breathing new life into the French economy: he appointed Physiocrat Robert Turgot as Controller General of Finance. The Physiocrats were a small band of followers of the French physician François Quesnay, whose economic prescriptions included reduced taxes, less regulation, the elimination of government-granted monopolies and internal tolls and tariffs—ideas that found their rallying cry in the famous slogan, "laissez-faire, laissez-passer."

The Physiocrats exerted a profound influence on Adam Smith, who had spent time in France in the 1760s and whose classic *The Wealth of Nations* embodied the Physiocratic attack on mercantilism and argued that nations get rich by practicing free trade.[2] Of Smith, Turgot, and the Physiocrats, the great French statesman and author Frederic Bastiat (1801–1850) wrote: "The basis of their whole economic system may be truly said to lie in the principle of self-interest. . . . The only function of government according to this doctrine is to protect life, liberty, and property."[3]

Embracing the principle of free trade not just as a temporary expedient, but as a philosophy, Turgot got the king to sign an edict in January 1776 that abolished the monopolies and special privileges of the guilds, corporations, and trading companies. He also abolished the forced labor of the peasants on the roads, the hated *corvée*. He then dedicated himself to breaking down the internal tariffs within France. By limiting government expense, he was able to cut the budget by 60 million livres and reduce the interest on the national debt from 8.7 million livres to 3 million livres.

Had Turgot been allowed to pursue his policies of free trade and less government intervention, France might very well have become Europe's first "common market" and avoided violent revolution. A rising tide would have lifted all ships. Unfortunately for France and the cause of freedom, resistance from the Court and special interests proved too powerful, and Turgot was removed from office in 1776. "The dismissal of this great man," wrote Voltaire, "crushes me. . . .

Since that fatal day, I have not followed anything . . . and am waiting patiently for someone to cut our throats."[4] Turgot's successors, following a mercantilist policy of government intervention, only made the French economy worse. In a desperate move to find money in the face of an uproar across the country and to re-establish harmony Louis XVI agreed to convene the Estates General for May 1789. Meanwhile, the king's new finance minister, Jacques Necker, a Swiss financial expert, delayed the effects of mercantilism by importing large amounts of grain.

On May 5, the Estates-General convened at Versailles. By June 17, the Third Estate had proclaimed itself the National Assembly. Three days later, the delegates took the famous Tennis Court Oath, vowing not to disband until France had a new constitution.

But the real French Revolution began not at Versailles but on the streets of Paris. On July 14, a Parisian mob attacked the old fortress known as the Bastille, liberating, as one pundit put it, "two fools, four forgers and a debaucher." The Bastille was no longer being used as a political prison, and Louis XVI had even made plans to destroy it. That made little difference to the mob, who were actually looking for weapons.

Promising the guards safe conduct if they surrendered, the leaders of the mob broke their word and hacked them to death. It would be the first of many broken promises. Soon the heads, torsos, and hands of the Bastille's former guardians were bobbing along the street on pikes. "In all," as historian Otto Scott put it, "a glorious victory of unarmed citizens over the forces of tyranny, or so the newspapers and history later said."[5] The French Revolution had begun.

Despite the bloodshed at the Bastille and the riots in Paris, there was some clear-headed thinking. Mirabeau wanted to keep the Crown but restrain it. "We need a government like England's," he said.[6] But the French not only hated things English, they even began to despise their own cultural heritage—the good as well as the bad. On October 5, the Assembly adopted the Declaration of the Rights of Man and the Citizen—a good document all right, but only if it were followed.

Twenty-eight days later, the Assembly showed they had no intention of doing so: all church property in France was confiscated by the government. It was the wrong way to go about creating a free society. Certainly the Church was responsible for some abuses, but seeking to build a free society by undermining property rights is like cutting down trees to grow a forest. Such confiscation only sets a precedent for further violation of property rights, which in turn violates individual rights—the very rights of man and the citizen the new government was so loudly proclaiming. By confiscating church property—no matter how justified—France's Revolutionary leaders showed that they weren't interested in a truly free society, only in one created in the image of their own philosophers. As Bastiat later pointed out, they were among the modern world's first social engineers.

Soon France began to descend into an abyss in which it would remain for the next 25 years. In towns where royalist mayors were still popular, bands of men invaded town halls and killed city magistrates. Thousands of people sold their homes and fled the country, taking with them precious skills and human capital. François Babeuf, the first modern communist, created a Society of Equals dedicated to the abolition of private property and the destruction of all those who held property. The king's guards were eventually captured and killed. The Marquis de Sade, from whom we get the term sadism, was released from prison. The Paris Commune took over control of Paris.

Fiat Money Inflation

The actions of the government were even more radical than those of the people at large. In order to meet the continuing economic crisis, the Assembly resorted to paper money—the infamous assignats, backed ostensibly by the confiscated church property. Although most of the delegates were aware of the dangers of paper money, it was thought that if the government issued only a small amount—and that backed up by the confiscated property—the assignats would not create the kind of economic disaster that had accompanied the use of paper money in the past.

But as had happened again and again through history, the government proved unable to discipline itself. As Andrew Dickson White put it in his *Fiat Money Inflation in France:* "New issues of paper were then clamored for as more drams are demanded by a drunkard. New issues only increased the evil; capitalists were all the more reluctant to embark their money on such a sea of doubt. Workmen of all sorts were more and more thrown out of employment. Issue after issue of currency came; but no relief resulted save a momentary stimulus which aggravated the disease."[7]

Writing from England in 1790, long before the French inflation had done its worst, Edmund Burke saw the danger of fiat currency. According to Burke, issuing assignats was the government's pat answer to any problem: "Is there a debt which presses them? Issue assignats. Are compensations to be made or a maintenance decreed to those whom they have robbed of their free-hold in their office, or expelled from their profession? Assignats. Is a fleet to be fitted out? Assignats. . . . Are the old assignats depreciated at market? What is the remedy? Issue new assignats." The leaders of France, said Burke, were like quack doctors who urged the same remedy for every illness.

Burke saw in the French Revolution not a decrease in the power of the state, but an increase in it: "The establishment of a system of liberty would of course be supposed to give it [France's currency] new strength; and so it would actually have done if a system of liberty had been established." As for the confiscation of property—first that of the Catholic Church then that of anyone accused of being an enemy of the Revolution—Burke said: "Never did a state, in any case, enrich itself by the confiscation of the citizens."[8]

But the issuing of assignats was only the beginning. In the spring of 1792, the first Committee of Public Safety was established, charged with judging and punishing traitors. Soon the streets of Paris began to run with blood, as thousands of people were killed by the guillotine. The following fall, the French government announced that it was prepared to help subject peoples everywhere win their freedom. Thus, instead of peacefully exporting French products and French ideas on liberty, the French began exporting war and revolution . . . hence the saying, "When France sneezes, the whole world catches cold."

As more soldiers were needed to "liberate" the rest of Europe, France instituted history's first universal levy—the ultimate in state control over the lives of its citizens. Meanwhile, for opposing the Revolution, most of the city of Lyons was destroyed. And Lafayette, who at first had embraced the Revolution, was arrested as a traitor.

Stifling Controls

Soon a progressive income tax was passed, prices on grain were fixed, and the death penalty was meted out to those who refused to sell at the government's prices. Every citizen was required to carry an identity card issued by his local commune, called, in an Orwellian twist

Edmund Burke
(1729–1797)

of language, Certificates of Good Citizenship. Every house had to post an outside listing of its legal occupants; the Revolutionary Communes had committees that watched everyone in the neighborhood; and special passes were needed to travel from one city to another. The jails were soon filled with more people than they had been under Louis XVI. Eventually, there flooded forth such a torrent of laws that virtually every citizen was technically guilty of crimes against the state. The desire for absolute equality resulted in everyone's being addressed as "citizen," much as the modern-day Communist is referred to as "comrade."

Education was centralized and bureaucratized. The old traditions, dialects, and local allegiances that helped prevent centralization—and thus tyranny—were swept away as the Assembly placed a mathematical grid of departments, cantons, and municipalities on an unsuspecting France. Each department was to be run exactly as its neighbor. Since "differences" were aristocratic, plans were made to erase individual cultures, dialects, and customs. In order to accomplish this, teachers—paid by the state—began to teach a uniform language. Curriculum was controlled totally by the central government. Summing up this program, Saint-Just said, "Children belong to the State," and advocated taking boys from their families at the age of five.[9]

So much of modern statism—with all of its horror and disregard for individualism—began with the French Revolution. The "purge," the "commune," the color red as a symbol of statism, even the political terms Left, Right, and Center came to us from this period. The only thing that ended the carnage—inside France, at least—was "a man on horseback," Napoleon Bonaparte. The French Revolution had brought forth first anarchy, then statism, and finally, dictatorship. Had it not been for the indomitable spirit of the average Frenchman and France's position as the largest country in Western Europe, France might never have recovered.

Now contrast all of this with the American Revolution—more correctly called the War for Independence. The American Revolution was different because, as Irving Kristol has pointed out, it was "a mild and relatively bloodless revolution. A war was fought to be sure, and soldiers died in that war. But . . . there was none of the butchery which we have come to accept as a natural concomitant of revolutionary warfare. . . . There was no 'revolutionary justice'; there was no reign of terror; there were no bloodthirsty proclamations by the Continental Congress."[10]

A "Conservative Revolution"

The American Revolution was essentially a "conservative" movement, fought to conserve the freedoms America had painstakingly developed since the 1620s during the period of British "salutary neglect"—in reality, a period of laissez-faire government as far as the colonies were concerned. Samuel Eliot Morison has pointed out: "[T]he American Revolution was not fought to *obtain* freedom, but to *preserve* the liberties that Americans already had as colonials. Independence was no conscious goal, secretly nurtured in cellar or jungle by bearded conspirators, but a reluctant last resort, to preserve 'life, liberty, and the pursuit of happiness.'"[11]

A sense of restraint pervaded this whole period. In the Boston Tea Party, no one was hurt and no property was damaged save for the tea.

One patriot even returned the next day to replace a lock on a sea chest that had been accidentally broken.[12] This was not the work of anarchists who wanted to destroy everything in their way, but of Englishmen who simply wanted a redress of grievances.

After the Boston Massacre, when the British soldiers who had fired upon the crowd were brought to trial, they were defended by American lawyers James Otis and John Adams. In any other "revolution," these men would have been calling for the deaths of the offending soldiers. Instead, they were defending them in court.

When the war finally began, it took over a year for the colonists to declare their independence. During that year, officers in the Continental Army still drank to "God save the King." When independence was finally declared, it was more out of desperation than careful planning, as the colonists sought help from foreign nations, particularly the French. In the end, it was the French monarchy—not the Revolutionists, as they had not yet come to power—that helped America win its independence.

Through the seven years of the American war, there were no mass executions, no "reigns of terror," no rivers of blood flowing in the streets of America's cities. When a Congressman suggested to George Washington that he raid the countryside around Valley Forge to feed his starving troops, he flatly refused, saying that such an action would put him on the same level as the invaders.

Most revolutions consume those who start them; in France, Marat, Robespierre, and Danton all met violent deaths. But when Washington was offered a virtual dictatorship by some of his officers at Newburgh, New York, he resisted his natural impulse to take command and urged them to support the republican legislative process. Professor Andrew C. McLaughlin has pointed out: "To teach our youth and persuade ourselves that the heroes of the controversy were only those taking part in tea-parties and various acts of violence is to inculcate the belief that liberty and justice rest in the main upon lawless force. And yet as a matter of plain fact, the self-restraint of the colonists is the striking theme; and their success in actually establishing institutions under which we still live was a remarkable achievement. No one telling the truth about the Revolution will attempt to conceal the fact that there was disorder.... [Yet] we find it marked on the whole by constructive political capacity."[13]

No Assault on Freedom of Religion

In America, unlike France, where religious dissenters were put to death, there was no wholesale assault on freedom of religion. At the Constitutional Convention in 1787, there were devout Congregationalists, Episcopalians, Dutch Reformed, Lutherans, Quakers, Presbyterians, Methodists, and Roman Catholics. Deist Ben Franklin asked for prayer during the Convention, while several months later George Washington spoke at a synagogue. During the Revolution, many members of the Continental Congress attended sermons preached by Presbyterian John Witherspoon, and while Thomas Jefferson worked to separate church and state in Virginia, he personally raised money to help pay the salaries of Anglican ministers who would lose their tax-supported paychecks. In matters of religion, the leaders of America's Revolution agreed to disagree.

Finally, unlike the French Revolution, the American Revolution brought forth what would become one of the world's freest societies. There were, of course, difficulties. During the "critical period" of American history, from 1783 to 1787, the 13 states acted as 13 separate nations, each levying import duties as it pleased. As far as New York was concerned, tariffs could be placed on New Jersey cider, produced across the river, as easily as on West Indian rum. The war had been won, but daily battles in the marketplace were being lost.

The U.S. Constitution changed all that by forbidding states to levy tariffs against one another. The result was, as John Chamberlain put it in his history of American business, "the greatest 'common market' in history."[14] The Constitution also sought to protect property rights, including rights to ideas (patents and copyrights) and beliefs (the First Amendment). For Madison, this was indeed the sole purpose of civil government. In 1792 he wrote: "Government is instituted to protect property of every sort.... This being the end of government, that alone is a just government which *impartially* secures to every man whatever is his own."[15] Alexander Hamilton, the first Secretary of the Treasury, helped restore faith in the public credit with his economic program. It was at his urging that the U.S. dollar was defined in terms of hard money—silver and gold. (At the Constitutional Convention, the delegates were so opposed to fiat paper money that Luther Martin of Maryland complained that they were "filled with paper money dread.")

Hamilton's centralizing tendencies would have been inappropriate at any other time in American history; but in the 1790s, his program helped 13 nations combine to form one United States. Had succeeding Treasury Secretaries continued Hamilton's course of strengthening the federal government, at the expense of the states, America's economic expansion would have been stillborn.

Fortunately, when Jefferson came to power he brought with him the Swiss financier and economist Albert Gallatin, who served Jefferson for two terms and Madison for one. Unlike his fellow countryman Necker, whose mercantilist policies only hastened the coming of the French Revolution, Gallatin was committed to limited government and free market economic policies. Setting the tone for his Administration, Jefferson said in his first inaugural address: "Still one thing more, fellow citizens—a wise and frugal government, which shall restrain men from injuring one another, shall leave them otherwise free to regulate their own pursuits of industry and improvement, and shall not take from the mouth of labor the bread it has earned."

For the next eight years, Jefferson and Gallatin worked to reduce the nation's debt as well as its taxes. The national debt was cut from $83 million to $57 million, and the number of federal employees was reduced. Despite the restrictions on trade caused by Napoleon's Berlin and Milan decrees, and the British blockade of Europe, American businessmen continued to develop connections around the world. By the end of Jefferson's first term, he was able to ask "What farmer, what mechanic, what laborer ever sees a tax gatherer in the United States?"[16] By 1810, America was well on its way to becoming the world's greatest economic power. France, meanwhile, still languished under the heavy hand of Napoleon.

In his Report to the House of Representatives that same year, Gallatin summed up the reasons for America's prosperity: "No cause . . . has perhaps more promoted in every respect the general prosperity of the United States than the absence of those systems of internal restrictions and monopoly which continue to disfigure the state of society in other countries. No law exists here directly or indirectly confining man to a particular occupation or place, or excluding any citizen from any branch he may at any time think proper to pursue. Industry is in every respect perfectly free and unfettered; every species of trade, commerce, art, profession, and manufacture being equally opened to all without requiring any previous regular apprenticeship,

Albert Gallatin
(1761–1849)

admission, or license."[17] The American Revolution was followed by 200 years of economic growth under the same government. By contrast, the French Revolution was followed by political instability including three revolutions, a directorate, a Reign of Terror, a dictatorship, a restoration of the Bourbon Monarchy, another monarchy, and five republics. Today, socialism has a greater hold in France than it does in America—although America is not far behind. Even though they were close in time, it was the French Revolution that set the pattern for the Russian Revolution and other modern revolutions, not the American.

Bastiat's Opinion

Frederic Bastiat clearly saw the difference between the two. The French Revolution, he argued, was based on the idea of Rousseau that society is contrary to nature, and therefore must be radically changed.

Because, according to Rousseau, the "social contract" had been violated early in man's history, it allowed all parties to that contract to return to a state of "natural liberty." In essence, what Rousseau was saying was, "Sweep aside all the restraints of property and society, destroy the existing system. Then you will be free, free to lose yourself in the collective good of mankind, under my care."[18]

The social architects who emerged out of the chaos of the French Revolution included Robespierre and Napoleon. In his analysis of Robespierre, Bastiat said: "Note that when Robespierre demands a dictatorship, it is . . . to make his own moral principles prevail by means of terror. . . . Oh, you wretches! . . . You want to reform everything! Reform yourselves first! This will be enough of a task for you."[19]

In Bastiat's opinion, the French Revolution failed because it repudiated the very principles upon which a free society is based: self-government, property rights, free markets, and limited civil government. The American Revolution, however, brought forth the world's freest society: "Look at the United States," wrote Bastiat. "There is no country in the world where the law confines itself more rigorously to its proper role, which is to guarantee every one's liberty and property. Accordingly, there is no country in which the social order seems to rest on a more stable foundation. . . . This is how they understand freedom and democracy in the United States. There each citizen is vigilant with a jealous care to remain his own master. It is by virtue of such freedom that the poor hope to emerge from poverty, and that the rich hope to preserve their wealth. And, in fact, as we see, in a very short time this system has brought the Americans to a degree of enterprise, security, wealth, and equality of which the annals of the human race offer no other example. . . . [In America] each person can in full confidence dedicate his capital and his labor to production. He does not have to fear that his plans and calculations will be upset from one instant to another by the legislature."[20]

Bastiat did see two inconsistencies in the American Republic: slavery ("a violation of the rights of a person") and tariffs ("a violation of the right to property"). According to Bastiat, these were the two issues that would divide America if they were not dealt with speedily.

What was the answer for America as well as France? "Be responsible for ourselves," said Bastiat. "Look to the State for nothing beyond law and order. Count on it for no wealth, no enlightenment. No more holding it responsible for our faults, our negligence, our improvidence. Count only on ourselves for our subsistence, our physical, intellectual, and moral progress!"[21]

On the 200th anniversary of the French Revolution, Frenchmen and Americans can truly become partners in liberty by working toward the principles advocated by Bastiat, America's Founding Fathers, and others: limited government, private property, free markets, and free men.

---

1. Piotr Kropotkin, *The Great French Revolution* (New York: Putnam's Sons, 1909), introduction.

2. So strong were the connections between the Physiocrats and Adam Smith that, according to the French economists Charles Gide and Charles Rist, "But for the death of Quesnay in 1774 two years before the publication of *The Wealth of Nations*—Smith would have dedicated his masterpiece to him." Later, Frederic Bastiat grouped Smith, Quesnay, and Turgot together as "my guides and masters." Dean Russell, *Frederic Bastiat Ideas and Influence* (Irvington-on-Hudson, N.Y.: The Foundation for Economic Education, 1969), pp. 58, 19.

3. Russell, p. 20.

4. Peter Gay and R. K. Webb, *Modern Europe to 1815* (New York: Harper and Row, 1973), p. 462.

5. Otto J. Scott, *Robespierre: The Voice of Virtue* (New York: Mason and Lipscomb Publishers, 1974), pp. 59–61.

6. *Ibid.,* p. 54.

7. Andrew Dickson White, *Fiat Money Inflation in France* (Irvington-on-Hudson, N.Y.: The Foundation for Economic Education, 1959), p. 107.

8. Edmund Burke, *Reflections on the Revolution in France* (Indianapolis: The Bobbs-Merrill Co., 1955, originally published in 1790), pp. 275–276, 280.

9. Scott, pp. 223–224.

10. Benjamin Hart, *Faith and Freedom* (Dallas: Lewis and Stanley, 1988), p. 301.

11. Samuel Eliot Morison, *The Oxford History of the American People* (New York: Oxford University Press, 1965), p. 182.

12. Gene Fisher and Glen Chambers, *The Revolution Myth* (Greenville, S.C.: Bob Jones University Press, 1981), p. 18.

13. Andrew C. McLaughlin, *The Foundations of American Constitutionalism* (New York: Fawcett [1932], 1961), pp. 88–89.

14. John Chamberlain, *The Enterprising Americans: A Business History of the United States* (New York: Harper and Row Publishers [1974], 1981), p. 37.

15. *Letters and Other Writings of James Madison* (New York: R. Worthington, 1884), IV, p. 478.

16. James Richardson, ed., *A Compilation of the Messages and Papers of the Presidents* (New York: Bureau of National Literature, 1897), I, p. 367.

17. John M. Blum, et al., *The National Experience Part I* (New York: Harcourt Brace Jovanovich [1963], 1981), p. 213.

18. George Charles Roche, *Frederic Bastiat: A Man Alone* (New Rochelle, N.Y.: Arlington House, 1971), pp. 146–147.

19. *Ibid.,* p. 148.

20. *Ibid.,* pp. 205–206, 244.

21. *Ibid.,* p. 164.

George Washington on Liberty and Order

by Clarence B. Carson

There are truths to which the passage of time and the gaining of experience add luster and vitality. So it has been, for me at least, with those contained in Washington's Farewell Address. With each reading of it, I have been impressed anew with the relevance of so much that he had to say to our own time. Often, too, I discover some new theme or emphasis that I had not been aware of earlier. Undoubtedly, these different impressions arise in part from the richness of the material but also may be conditioned by my particular interests at a given time. At any rate, the theme of liberty and order stood out for me in my latest reading of the Farewell Address. It seemed to me that all the parts fitted together into a whole within the framework of this theme.

Before getting into that, however, it may be of some aid to place the address in a much broader historical frame. Some observations about liberty and order more generally will help to set the stage for his remarks.

Thoughtful men may differ about the desirability of liberty, but they rarely do about the necessity for order. Also, nations, kingdoms, and empires have differed much more over the extent of liberty within them than of the degree of order, over long periods of time anyway. They have ranged from the most compulsive tyrannies to ones in which considerable liberty prevails. By contrast, all governments are to a greater or lesser extent devoted to maintaining order. But there are great differences of belief, persuasion, and practice as to how order is to be maintained and the proper role of government in doing so. These differences largely determine the extent of liberty in a country.

There have been, and are, countries in which those in power be-

---

Dr. Carson has written and taught extensively, specializing in American intellectual history. He is the author of several books, including *A Basic History of the United States,* a five-volume narrative history. This article is reprinted from the February 1983 issue of *The Freeman.*

lieve that government must act to impose order in every nook and cranny of society. The active principle in this, if principle it be, is that if government does not impose order then disorder and chaos will prevail. Thomas Hobbes, English philosopher in the seventeenth century, expressed this view with clarity and force. He declared that if men were permitted to act according "to their particular judgments and particular appetites, they can expect thereby no defense, nor protection against a common enemy, nor against the injuries of one another." There must be a power over them, he said, and the way to get that power is "to confer all their power and strength upon one man, or upon one assembly of men, that may reduce all their wills . . . unto one will. . . . For by this authority, given him by every particular man in the commonwealth, he hath the use of so much power and strength conferred on him, that by terror thereof, he is enabled to perform the wills of them all. . . ."

A view similar to this of what was necessary to order and how it could be achieved, as well as the role of government in it, was widespread in Europe in the seventeenth century. It was an age of royal absolutism, claims about the Divine right kings, and of the assertion of government power to direct the lives of peoples. England had an established church; no others were tolerated. All were required to attend its services, contribute to its support, and have most of the great events of life celebrated or recorded in it. The church officials censored publications, licensed schools, and kept watch over the doings of the people.

Mercantilism

Economic life was circumscribed and controlled by the government under a system most commonly known as mercantilism. The government controlled exports and imports, gave subsidies, bounties, and grants to encourage certain undertakings, prohibited others, gave patents, charters, and other forms of monopolies to individuals and companies, enforced craft regulations and maintained much power over the lands of the realm. Harsh penalties were imposed for every sort of offense from blasphemy to treason. Evidence abounded that government was making massive efforts to impose order. As for liberties, they had most commonly to be asserted against the grain of the prevailing system.

So, too, in the twentieth century the dominant view of those in power in many lands is that government must impose an all-encompassing order upon the peoples under its sway. At its farthest reaches, this view achieves its fruition in the totalitarian state, with its direct control over all the media of communication, every aspect of the economy, over education, over such religion as is permitted, over work and over play.

In other lands, where this bent toward state-compelled order has been moderated thus far—has been kept from going so far—it evinces itself in government intervention in the economy, the thrust of regulation into many realms, in redistribution of the wealth, in controls over education, medicine, charity, and hundreds of other areas. The ideologies supporting this pervasive government power differ in many particular respects from those that supported seventeenth-century government power, but the notion that government must impose an order else chaos and disorder will prevail is common to both. Extensive liberty can hardly be reconciled with such compulsive orders.

That George Washington held a view on how to maintain order and the proper role of government in sharp contrast to those described above is manifest in his life and works. Moreover, a seismic change in outlook, both in England and America and over much of Europe, had taken place between the time when Hobbes had penned his *Leviathan* and the founding of the United States. A major aspect of that change was a shift from the emphasis upon a government order imposed on men toward individual liberty and responsibility. The shift sparked in many Americans an awareness of the danger of government both to liberty and to order. At the root of this shift was a different conception of the origin and nature of order.

Belief in a Natural Order

George Washington and his contemporaries were imbued with a strong belief in a natural order. Order, in their view, was not something that could be arbitrarily contrived and imposed by man. The foundations of order, they held, are in the frame of the universe, in the laws that govern it, in the nature of man and his faculty of reason, and in the principles of relationships by which constructive activities can take place. At best, men can only act in accord with and imitate the order that is given.

George Washington
(1732–1799)

The belief in a natural law and natural order was not new to the eighteenth century, of course; it had been around since the ancient Greeks and Romans, at least. But it had come to the forefront in the century before the founding of the United States as a result both of vigorous efforts to revive it and of many scientific and philosophical formulations of it.

Newton had persuasively set forth in mathematical terms the laws governing the course of the heavenly bodies. Thinkers were getting impressive results in their searches for the laws and principles governing all sorts of relationships. What struck so many in that age was the idea of proportion, balance, harmony, and order resident in the natural tendencies of the world about them. Most marvelous of all, at least to many, this order was consonant to human liberty. Rather than frustrating man in the use of his faculties for his benefit (and for the commonweal as well), the natural order provided means for him to do so most effectively. The foundations of liberty in this belief in a natural order were in the natural rights doctrine.

In his Farewell Address, Washington did not expand upon or elaborate on the theme of liberty. Although the word "liberty" occurs several times in the document, it plays mainly a supportive role in what he has to say. The attachment to liberty is assumed, a given if you will, upon which to hinge his arguments. Washington said as much himself: "Interwoven as is the love of liberty with every ligament of your hearts, no recommendation of mine is necessary to fortify or confirm the attachment." But, he says, from first one angle then another, if you would have liberty you must support those things on which it depends.

For example, in recommending a united support for the general government, he declared: "This Government, the offspring of our own choice,... adopted upon full investigation and mature deliberation, completely free in its principles, in the distribution of its power, uniting security with energy, and containing within itself a provision for its own amendment, has a just claim to your confidence and support." To clinch the argument, he says that these "are duties enjoined by the fundamental maxims of true liberty." In arguing against the involvement of Americans in foreign intrigues, he says that by doing so "they will avoid the necessity of those overgrown military establishments which, under any form of government, are inauspicious to liberty...."

A Sense of Order

The word "liberty" occurs frequently throughout the address, but by my fairly careful count the word "order" occurs only once. Even that instance is insignificant, however, for the word is used in a phrase, as "in order to" do something or other. It occurs at one other point as part of the word "disorders," which, while more significant, is hardly proof of a theme. Yet a sense of order pervades the whole document. It is there in the cadences of the sentences, in the matching of phrase with phrase, in the balance of one tendency against another, in the thrust toward discovering a common bond by piling up references to particular interests. It is clear, if one reads between the lines, that there is an order for men's lives, an order for nations, an order for relations among nations, an order by which parts belong to a whole, and an order by which balance and harmony can be maintained. Government is not the origin of this order, but it is necessary to the maintenance of it, even as it is ever a potential threat to it. Government is made necessary by the bent in man to disrupt order.

The two main sources of disorder to which Washington alludes are these. First, there are those passions in men which incline them to pursue their own particular and partisan designs at the expense of the well-being of others. Washington called it the spirit of parity, but we might understand it better as partisanship for causes. (He had in mind the dangers of this to the stability of government, but it does no violence to his idea to apply it to individuals as well as groups.) "This spirit," he said, "unfortunately, is inseparable from our nature, having its roots in the strongest passions of the human mind." Among the dangers of these partisan passions, he declared, are these: "It serves always to distract the public councils and enfeeble the public administration. It agitates the community with ill-founded jealousies and false alarms; kindles the animosity of one part against an other; foments occasionally riot and insurrection. It opens the door to foreign influence and corruption. . . . Thus the policy and will of one country are subjected to the policy and will of another."

The other source of disorder, to which Washington alludes, is "that love of power and proneness to abuse it which predominates in the human heart. . . ." It is this power hunger which makes government dangerous, for it prompts those who govern to overstep the bounds of their authority. "The spirit of encroachment," Washington pointed out, "tends to consolidate the powers of all the departments in one, and thus to create, whatever the form of government, a real despotism."

Advice and Counsel

The body of the Farewell Address is devoted to advice and counsel about how to conduct the government so as to maintain order and preserve liberty, and to warnings about holding in check those partisan tendencies and the bent toward consolidating power which endanger them. The following were his main points: (1) maintain the union; (2) keep the principles of the Constitution intact; (3) preserve national independence; (4) buttress policy and behavior with religion and morality; (5) cherish the public credit; and (6) follow peaceful policies toward all nations. These general principles are not nearly so revealing, however, as his particular recommendations and the arguments he used to support them.

The main device Washington employed to support his advice to maintain the union was to invoke those things the people had in common: the name "American," their struggles for independence, their common beliefs, and their common interest. He surveyed the continent, from a mountaintop as it were, and ticked off how north and south, east and west, were bound together.

"The *North,*" he said, "in an unrestrained intercourse with the South, protected by the equal laws of a common government, finds in the production of the latter great . . . resources of maritime and commercial enterprise and precious materials of manufacturing industry. The *South,* in the same intercourse . . . sees its agriculture grow and commerce expand. . . . The *East,* in a like intercourse with the *West,* already finds . . . a valuable vent for the commodities which it brings from abroad or manufactures at home. The *West* derives from the *East* supplies requisite to its growth and comfort." This was an economic order which had its roots in the diversities of regions. Washington warned against the rise of factions seeking to political power for partisan ends that might disrupt the union and disturb the existing order.

Preserve the Constitution

Washington's concern for preserving the Constitution intact was motivated by the belief that a balance had been incorporated in it, a balance in which the national and state government checked one another and the branches held one another in check. "The necessity of reciprocal checks in the exercise of political power," he declared, "by dividing and distributing it . . . has been evinced by experiments ancient and modern. . . ." "Liberty itself," he pointed out, "will find in such a government with powers properly distributed and adjusted, its surest guardian." He warned against two things in particular. One was the "spirit of innovation upon its principles." The other was "change by usurpation" of power. That was not to say that the Constitution was perfect as it stood in 1796. But if something needed correcting, it should be "by an amendment in the way which the Constitution designates." No man or body of men should assume the power to do so, "for though this in one instance may be the instrument of good, it is the customary weapon by which federal governments are destroyed." Washington hoped that the United States would follow an independent course in world affairs, that it would lend its weight toward an order in which peace would be the norm, but that it would not become entangled with other nations in the quest for power and dominance. His distrust of government did not end at the water's edge, for he believed that foreign governments would, if they could, use the United States for their own ends. He warned "Against the insidious wiles of foreign influence," for "(I conjure you to believe me, fellow-citizens) the jealousy of a free people ought to be *constantly* awake, since history and experience prove that foreign influence is one of the most baneful foes of republican government." Underlying these fears was the belief that in the nature of things, in the natural order, each nation pursues its own interests. Hence, "There can be no greater error than to expect or calculate upon real favors from nation to nation." He cautioned against constant preference for one nation and opposition to others. "It is our true policy," Washington said, "to steer clear of permanent alliances with any portion of the foreign world. . . ."

Religion and Morality

The first President had some other recommendations on foreign policy, but before discussing them, it would be best, as he did, to refer to the role of religion and morality. The belief in a natural order, the hope that the American political system had been shaped in accord with it, was not sufficient, in Washington's opinion, to assure the working or continuation of order among men. Man is a creature of unruly passions, as already noted, and the necessary corrective to these is religion and morality.

"It is substantially true," Washington commented, "that virtue or morality is a necessary spring of popular government." And, "Of all the dispositions and habits which lead to political prosperity, religion and morality are indispensable supports. In vain would that man claim the tribute of patriotism who should labor to subvert these great pillars of human happiness. . . . A volume could not trace all their connections with private and public felicity." Moreover, "let us with caution indulge the supposition that morality can be maintained without religion."

These remarks preceded both his advice on public credit and on peaceful relations with other nations. On cherishing the public credit, he said: "One method of preserving it is to use it as sparingly as possible. . . ." Washington expected that there would be occasions for extraordinary expenses, making war came to mind, when it might be necessary for the government to borrow money. But he warned against the "accumulation of debt," declaring that the way to avoid this was "not only by shunning occasions of expense, but by vigorous exertions in time of peace to discharge the debts which unavoidable wars have occasioned." That way, it should be possible to avoid "ungenerously throwing upon posterity the burthen which we ourselves ought to bear." Washington thought his countrymen might be the more inclined to follow these policies if they would keep in mind "that toward the payment of debts there must be revenue; that to have revenue there must be taxes; that no taxes can be devised which are not more or less inconvenient and unpleasant. . . ." Not everyone may find the balanced formulations of eighteenth-century sentences pleasant but it must be admitted that the logic in the above is impressive.

At any rate, the principles discussed in the above two paragraphs provided the framework for his recommendations for maintaining peaceful relations with other nations. To that end, Washington advised this: "Observe good faith and justice toward all nations. Cultivate peace and harmony with all. Religion and morality enjoin this conduct. And can it be that good policy does not equally enjoin it." Above all, "The great rule of conduct for us in regard to foreign nations is, in extending our commercial relations to have with them as little *political* connection as possible."

Any extended political connections—permanent alliances, for example—could only embroil the United States in the conflicts among other nations. Otherwise, "Harmony, liberal intercourse with nations are recommended by policy, humanity, and interest. But even our commercial policy should hold an equal and impartial hand, neither, seeking nor granting exclusive favors or preferences; consulting the natural course of things; diffusing and diversifying by gentle means the streams of commerce, but forcing nothing. . . ." That is surely the natural order for trade, and a plausible hope for peace to those who knew of, when they had not experienced, the devastating mercantile wars resulting from the use of force in national commerce.

A Farewell Message of Timeless Truths on Liberty and Order

George Washington reckoned that he had devoted the better part of forty-five years to the service of his country when he retired. He was an unabashed patriot, proud to be called an American, a sturdy friend of the union, and none knew better than he the struggles out of which the United States had been born. He was a man of his time, as are all mortal men, spoke in the phraseology of times past, yet in his Farewell Address he touched upon and elaborated some timeless truths. Further experience has served only to confirm the validity of many of his recommendations.

His thoughts on unity, on the love of power, on the impact of partisan strife, on the importance of focusing on our common interests, on avoiding entanglements with other nations, on religion and morality, on the public credit, and on freedom of trade have worn well when they have been observed, and have brought suffering by their neglect. The terror and tyranny of this century, the slave labor camps and barbed-wire borders of nations with their fettered peoples prove once again that liberty depends upon order, and that if order is not founded upon and in accord with an underlying order it will tend to be nothing more than the will of the tyrant.

Not Yours to Give

by David Crockett

One day in the House of Representatives, a bill was taken up appropriating money for the benefit of a widow of a distinguished naval officer. Several beautiful speeches had been made in its support. The Speaker was just about to put the question when Crockett arose:

"Mr. Speaker—I have as much respect for the memory of the deceased, and as much sympathy for the sufferings of the living, if suffering there be, as any man in this House, but we must not permit our respect for the dead or our sympathy for a part of the living to lead us into an act of injustice to the balance of the living. I will not go into an argument to prove that Congress has no power to appropriate this money as an act of charity. Every member upon this floor knows it. We have the right, as individuals, to give away as much of our own money as we please in charity; but as members of Congress we have no right so to appropriate a dollar of the public money. Some eloquent appeals have been made to us upon the ground that it is a debt due the deceased. Mr. Speaker, the deceased lived long after the close of the war; he was in office to the day of his death, and I have never heard that the government was in arrears to him.

"Every man in this House knows it is not a debt. We cannot, without the grossest corruption, appropriate this money as the payment of a debt. We have not the semblance of authority to appropriate it as a charity. Mr. Speaker, I have said we have the right to give as much money of our own as we please. I am the poorest man on this floor. I cannot vote for this bill, but I will give one week's pay to the object, and if every member of Congress will do the same, it will amount to more than the bill asks."

He took his seat. Nobody replied. The bill was put upon its passage, and, instead of passing unanimously, as was generally supposed, and as, no doubt, it would, but for that speech, it received but few votes, and, of course, was lost.

Later, when asked by a friend why he had opposed the appropriation, Crockett gave this explanation:

From *The Life of Colonel David Crockett,* compiled by Edward S. Ellis (Philadelphia: Porter & Coates, 1884). Reprinted from *The Freeman,* August 1961.

"Several years ago I was one evening standing on the steps of the Capitol with some other members of Congress, when our attention was attracted by a great light over in Georgetown. It was evidently a large fire. We jumped into a hack and drove over as fast as we could. In spite of all that could be done, many houses were burned and many families made houseless, and, besides, some of them had lost all but the clothes they had on. The weather was very cold, and when I saw so many women and children suffering, I felt that something ought to be done for them. The next morning a bill was introduced appropriating $20,000 for their relief. We put aside all other business and rushed it through as soon as it could be done.

"The next summer, when it began to be time to think about the election, I concluded I would take a scout around among the boys of my district. I had no opposition there, but, as the election was some time off, I did not know what might turn up. When riding one day in a part of my district in which I was more of a stranger than any other, I saw a man in a field plowing and coming toward the road. I gauged my gait so that we should meet as he came to the fence. As he came up, I spoke to the man. He replied politely, but, as I thought, rather coldly.

"I began: 'Well, friend, I am one of those unfortunate beings called candidates, and—'

"'Yes, I know you; you are Colonel Crockett. I have seen you once before, and voted for you the last time you were elected. I suppose you are out electioneering now, but you had better not waste your time or mine. I shall not vote for you again.'

"This was a sockdolager.... I begged him to tell me what was the matter.

"'Well, Colonel, it is hardly worth-while to waste time or words upon it. I do not see how it can be mended, but you gave a vote last winter which shows that either you have not capacity to understand the Constitution, or that you are wanting in the honesty and firmness to be guided by it. In either case you are not the man to represent me. But I beg your pardon for expressing it in that way. I did not intend to avail myself of the privilege of the constituent to speak plainly to a candidate for the purpose of insulting or wounding you. I intend by it only to say that your understanding of the Constitution is very different from mine; and I will say to you what, but for my rudeness, I should not have said, that I believe you to be honest.... But an understanding of the Constitution different from mine I cannot overlook, because the Constitution, to be worth anything, must be held sacred, and rigidly observed in all its provisions. The man who wields power and misinterprets it is the more dangerous the more honest he is.'

"'I admit the truth of all you say, but there must be some mistake about it, for I do not remember that I gave any vote last winter upon any Constitutional question.'

"'No, Colonel, there's no mistake. Though I live here in the backwoods and seldom go from home, I take the papers from Washington and read very carefully all the proceedings of Congress. My papers say that last winter you voted for a bill to appropriate $20,000 to some sufferers by a fire in Georgetown. Is that true?'

"'Well, my friend; I may as well own up. You have got me there. But certainly nobody will complain that a great and rich country like ours should give the insignificant sum of $20,000 to relieve its suffering women and children, particularly with a full and overflowing Treasury, and I am sure, if you had been there, you would have done just as I did.'

"'It is not the amount, Colonel, that I complain of; it is the principle. In the first place, the government ought to have in the Treasury no more than enough for its legitimate purposes. But that has nothing to do with the question. The power of collecting and disbursing money at pleasure is the most dangerous power that can be intrusted to man, particularly under our system of collecting revenue by a tariff, which reaches every man in the country, no matter how poor he may be, and the poorer he is the more he pays in proportion to his means. What is worse, it presses upon him without his knowledge where the weight centers, for there is not a man in the United States who can ever guess how much he pays to the government. So you see, that while you are contributing to relieve one, you are drawing it from thousands who are even worse off than he. If you had the right to give anything, the amount was simply a matter of discretion with you, and you had as much right to give $20,000,000 as $20,000. If you have the right to give to one, you have the right to give to all; and, as the Constitution neither defines charity nor stipulates the amount, you are at liberty to give to any and everything which you may believe, or profess to believe, is a charity, and to any amount you may think proper. You will very easily perceive what a wide door this would open for fraud and corruption and favoritism, on the one hand, and for robbing the people on the other. No, Colonel, Congress has no right to give charity. Individual members may give as much of their own money as they please, but they have no right to touch a dollar of the public money for that purpose. If twice as many houses had been burned in this county as in Georgetown, neither you nor any other member of Congress would have thought of appropriating a dollar for our relief. There are about two hundred and forty members of Congress. If they had shown their sympathy for the sufferers by contributing each one week's pay, it would have made over $13,000. There are plenty of wealthy men in and around Washington who could have given $20,000 without depriving themselves of even a luxury of life. The congressmen chose to keep their own money, which, if reports be true, some of them spend not very creditably; and the people about Washington, no doubt, applauded you for relieving them from the necessity of giving by giving what was not yours to give. The people have delegated to Congress, by the Constitution, the power to do certain things. To do these, it is authorized to collect and pay moneys, and for nothing else. Everything beyond this is usurpation, and a violation of the Constitution.

"'So you see, Colonel, you have violated the Constitution in what I consider a vital point. It is a precedent fraught with danger to the country, for when Congress once begins to stretch its power beyond the limits of the Constitution, there is no limit to it, and no security for the people. I have no doubt you acted honestly, but that does not make it any better, except as far as you are personally concerned, and you see that I cannot vote for you.'

"I tell you I felt streaked. I saw if I should have opposition, and this man should go to talking, he would set others to talking, and in that district I was a gone fawn-skin. I could not answer him, and the fact is, I was so fully convinced that he was right, I did not want to. But I must satisfy him, and I said to him:

"'Well, my friend, you hit the nail upon the head when you said I had not sense enough to understand the Constitution. I intended to he guided by it, and thought I had studied it fully. I have heard many speeches in Congress about the powers of Congress, but what you have said here at your plow has got more hard, sound sense in it than all the fine speeches I ever heard. If I had ever taken the view of it that you have, I would have put my head into the fire before I would have given that vote; and if you will forgive me and vote for me again, if I ever vote for another unconstitutional law I wish I may be shot.'

"He laughingly replied: 'Yes, Colonel, you have sworn to that once before, but I will trust you again upon one condition. You say that you are convinced that your vote was wrong. Your acknowledgment of it will do more good than beating you for it. If, as you go around the district, you will tell people about this vote, and that you are satisfied it was wrong, I will not only vote for you, but will do what I can to keep down opposition, and, perhaps, I may exert some little influence in that way.'

"'If I don't,' said I, 'I wish I may be shot; and to convince you that I am in earnest in what I say I will come back this way in a week or ten days, and if you will get up a gathering of the people, I will make a speech to them. Get up a barbecue, and I will pay for it.'

"'No, Colonel, we are not rich people in this section, but we have plenty of provisions to contribute for a barbecue, and some to spare for those who have none. The push of crops will be over in a few days, and we can then afford a day for a barbecue. This is Thursday; I will see to getting it up on Saturday week. Come to my house on Friday, and we will go together, and I promise you a very respectable crowd to see and hear you.'

"'Well, I will be here. But one thing more before I say good-by. I must know your name.'

"'My name is Bunce.'

"'Not Horatio Bunce?'

"'Yes.'

"'Well, Mr. Bunce, I never saw you before, though you say you have seen me, but I know you very well. I am glad I have met you, and very proud that I may hope to have you for my friend.'

"It was one of the luckiest hits of my life that I met him. He mingled but little with the public, but was widely known for his remarkable intelligence and incorruptible integrity, and for a heart brimful and running over with kindness and benevolence, which showed themselves not only in words but in acts. He was the oracle of the whole country around him, and his fame had extended far beyond the circle of his immediate acquaintance. Though I had never met him before, I had heard much of him, and but for this meeting it is very

Davy Crockett
(1786–1836)

likely I should have had opposition, and had been beaten. One thing is very certain, no man could now stand up in that district under such a vote.

"At the appointed time I was at his house, having told our conversation to every crowd I had met, and to every man I stayed all night with, and I found that it gave the people an interest and a confidence in me stronger than I had ever seen manifested before.

"Though I was considerably fatigued when I reached his house, and, under ordinary circumstances, should have gone early to bed, I kept him up until midnight, talking about the principles and affairs of government, and got more real, true knowledge of them than I had got all my life before.

"I have known and seen much of him since, for I respect him—no, that is not the word—I reverence and love him more than any living man, and I go to see him two or three times every year; and I will tell you, sir, if every one who professes to be a Christian lived and acted and enjoyed it as he does, the religion of Christ would take the world by storm.

"But to return to my story. The next morning we went to the barbecue, and, to my surprise, found about a thousand men there. I met a good many whom I had not known before, and they and my friend introduced me around until I had got pretty well acquainted—at least, they all knew me.

"In due time notice was given that I would speak to them. They gathered up around a stand that had been erected. I opened my speech by saying:

"'Fellow-citizens—I present myself before you today feeling like a new man. My eyes have lately been opened to truths which ignorance or prejudice, or both, had heretofore hidden from my view. I feel that I can today offer you the ability to render you more valuable service than I have ever been able to render before. I am here today more for the purpose of acknowledging my error than to seek your votes. That I should make this acknowledgment is due to myself as well as to you. Whether you will vote for me is a matter for your consideration only.'

"I went on to tell them about the fire and my vote for the appropriation and then told them why I was satisfied it was wrong. I closed by saying:

"'And now, fellow-citizens, it remains only for me to tell you that most of the speech you have listened to with so much interest was simply a repetition of the arguments by which your neighbor, Mr. Bunce, convinced me of my error.

"'It is the best speech I ever made in my life, but he is entitled to the credit for it. And now I hope he is satisfied with his convert and that he will get up here and tell you so.'

"He came upon the stand and said:

"'Fellow-citizens—It affords me great pleasure to comply with the request of Colonel Crockett. I have always considered him a thoroughly honest man, and I am satisfied that he will faithfully perform all that he has promised you today.'

"He went down, and there went up from that crowd such a shout for Davy Crockett as his name never called forth before.

"I am not much given to tears, but I was taken with a choking then and felt some big drops rolling down my cheeks. And I tell you now that the remembrance of those few words spoken by such a man, and the honest, hearty shout they produced, is worth more to me than all the honors I have received and all the reputation I have ever made, or ever shall make, as a member of Congress.

"Now, sir," concluded Crockett, "you know why I made that speech yesterday.

"There is one thing now to which I will call your attention. You remember that I proposed to give a week's pay. There are in that House many very wealthy men—men who think nothing of spending a week's pay, or a dozen of them, for a dinner or a wine party when they have something to accomplish by it. Some of those same men made beautiful speeches upon the great debt of gratitude which the country owed the deceased—a debt which could not be paid by money—and the insignificance and worthlessness of money, particularly so insignificant a sum as $10,000, when weighed against the honor of the nation. Yet not one of them responded to my proposition. Money with them is nothing but trash when it is to come out of the people. But it is the one great thing for which most of them are striving, and many of them sacrifice honor, integrity, and justice to obtain it."

II. TRIUMPH OF FREEDOM

The Robber Barons and the Real Gilded Age

by Edmund A. Opitz

The Civil War marks a deep cleavage in American life; the increasingly industrialized America of the latter decades of the nineteenth century was quite different from pre-Civil War America. The economy of the first part of the last century did of course engage in some manufacturing, but the businessman of the period was typically a merchant and a trader rather than a factory owner or mine operator. Men of ambition made money shipping lumber to China and returning with tea, opium, mandarin screens, and the like. American whalers plied their arduous trade all over the world. The Yankee clipper, sailing out of eastern ports from Baltimore to Salem, was the most beautiful thing afloat, and the swiftest vessel on the seven seas till after the Civil War.

Most Americans, during this period, lived in villages and small towns; farming was the major occupation, and rural life was a struggle for survival. Poverty was widespread, giving rise to the old New England maxim: Use it up, wear it out, make it do, or do without. Herman Melville's great novel *Moby Dick* tells how dirty and dangerous life was on board a whaling ship. Imagine then, if you will, what it was like trying to wrest a living out of the rocky soil of New England if life aboard a whaler was the preferred alternative!

No one would refer to the early decades of the last century as "The Era of Free Enterprise Individualism." It is the post-Civil War period that is usually labeled so. "Free Enterprise" and "Individualism" are two very slippery terms. In any event, the decades under evaluation here are bounded, on the one side, by the Presidency of Ulysses S. Grant, and on the other, by William McKinley—roughly from 1869 to 1901. This was America's Gilded Age, so labeled by Mark Twain in his novel of that name. *The Gilded Age* expressed Mark Twain's disillusionment over the decline in his nation from the decent, old, kindly America he remembered from his boyhood to the America of

---

The Reverend Mr. Opitz, an associate editor of *The Freeman,* was a senior staff member of The Foundation for Economic Education until his retirement in 1992. This article is reprinted from the August 1984 issue of *The Freeman*.

Black Friday, Credit Mobilier, Boss Tweed, Tammany, and the hustle for the fast buck.

The Changing Scene

Mark Twain, in collaboration with his neighbor Charles Dudley Warner—called "Deadly Warning" by his friends—published *The Gilded Age* in 1873. The theme of this novel is announced in the Preface: "In a State where there is no fever of speculation, no inflamed desire for sudden wealth, where the poor are all simple-minded and contented, and the rich are all honest and generous, where society is in a condition of primitive purity, and politics is the occupation of only the capable and the patriotic, there are necessarily no materials for such a history as we have constructed." But we no longer have people of this character, Mark Twain is telling us; corruption has eaten so deeply into the hearts and minds of people that he and Warner have ample material for the 453-page fictionalized history he and his friend have constructed.

In chapter 18 the authors venture a conjecture as to how this mutation in the American character had come about: "The eight years in America from 1860 to 1868 had uprooted institutions that were centuries old, changed the politics of a people, transformed the social life of half the country, and wrought so profoundly upon the entire national character that the influence cannot be measured short of two or three generations." The Gadarene progress was more rapid than Mark Twain had anticipated; it worked itself out close to the bitter end before he died thirty-seven years later.

Twain's satire was merely a prologue; the play followed, and the main characters are all well-known names. There were Thomas Durant and his friends on the Union Pacific, who grabbed federal subsidies and bribed Congressmen. There were Daniel Drew, Jim Fisk, and Jay Gould, the great stock manipulators. There were Huntington, Stanford, Cooke, Villard, Gary, and Morgan. I've listed here ten names; add more if you wish. The point is that these "robber barons," as they've been called, were a mere handful of men whose deeds and misdeeds have been lovingly chronicled by three generations of journalists and muckrakers.

Conniving with Politicians

These extravagant characters have been represented as exemplars of unrestrained individualism at its worst, fiercely competitive, practitioners of undiluted laissez-faire capitalism. They were nothing of the sort. So far were they from wanting a genuinely free market economy that they bought up senators and paid off judges in order to stifle competition. They did not want a government that would let them alone; they wanted a government they could use. Had they been able to understand the original idea of laissez faire they would have opposed it. They were not individualists; they did not believe in a fair field and no favor; they stacked the odds against their competitors.

The last thing Stanford, Gould, Gary, and the others wanted was open competition in a game where the best man wins. To the contrary! They connived with politicians to obtain advantages for themselves by controlling government and the law; they manipulated the public power for private gain. And the government was eager to oblige.

This was done openly, and virtually everyone knew about it. Witty commentators referred to certain politicians as the Senator from coal, or the Senator from railroads, or the Senator from steel. Oakes Ames, the president of the Union Pacific, dished out stock in the Credit Mobilier to obliging Congressmen in hopes of future favors. Such political practices were a far cry from the vision of James Madison, who had declared that "Justice is the end of government, and justice is the end of civil society." The Gilded Age was a throwback to the age-old practice of using political power for the economic advantage of those who hold office, and for their friends.

If you want the story of these men and their times, a good place to start is Gustavus Myers' *History of the Great American Fortunes*. First published in 1907, this book went through several editions here and in England. It was published in a large inexpensive edition in 1936 as a Modern Library Giant. I bought my secondhand copy in 1953; the original purchaser bought his in 1939 and it contains a gracious inscription by Myers himself: "May you be included in my next supplement to this tome."

Myers tells the reader that he was just a reformer when he began his research, eager to reveal the unsavory tactics of rapacious men in business and industry in the absence of government supervision of economic life. Only later did he conclude that a radical restructuring of society—some form of socialism—was the only answer. The conclusion is a strange one. Myers demonstrates throughout his book that such powers as government exercised in this nation during the Gilded Age were misused so as to wrongfully give monetary advantage to some at the expense of others. If this government with a little power did harm, there is no reason at all to assume that a new government wielding a lot of power will do good!

I have gone through Myers' book and underlined every passage which describes a sinister alliance between politicians and these fortune hunters; there are some hundred and fifty such passages. Let me offer you a representative sample.

> . . . peculiar special privileges, worth millions of dollars.
> . . . as a free gift from government.
> . . . the free use of the people's money, through the power of government.
> . . . a notorious violator of the law invoking the aid of the law to enrich himself still further.
> . . . causing public money to be turned over to his private treasury by either the tacit permission or connivance of government.
> . . . The simple mandate of law was sufficient authorization for them to prey upon the whole world outside their charmed circles.
> . . . while it was essential to control law-making bodies, it was imperative to have as their auxiliary the bodies [courts] that interpreted the law.

I think you catch the flavor of Mr. Myers' book. He is a moralist; he is indignant; he preaches a hell-fire and brimstone sermon against the wicked men who took advantage of their fellow Americans by subverting the law from its proper role of administering an evenhanded justice between person and person. They bent the law into an instrument of plunder. But Myers is not a philosopher; he does not shape his material according to a coherent theory of the economic and political orders.

Gaudy tales about these few unprincipled buccaneers distract our attention from the many legitimate entrepreneurs during the Gilded

Age who produced quality products at low prices with no federal subsidies. While Jay Gould was manipulating the Erie Railroad, Cornelius Vanderbilt was building a better line—the New York Central—with no help from government. John D. Rockefeller and James J. HIll climbed to the top of their fields by cutting costs, not throats. So did Charles Schwab and Henry Ford.

Also, we must not forget the millions of Americans on the farm and in the workshops. These hard-working people constituted the real American economy during the Gilded Age. This bustling, surging economy of ours received immigrants from Europe at a rate of about a million a year, and it absorbed them on our farms and in other places of work. The standard of living was rising all the while; wages doubled between 1870 and 1900.

It was an age of invention. During the eighty years from 1790 to 1870, the U.S. Patent Office had granted just over 40,000 patents; during the next thirty years it granted just over 400,000. New types of farm machinery transformed agriculture. To cite one instance: not one bushel of wheat had been raised in the Dakota Territory before 1881; by 1887 its wheat crop was sixty-two million bushels. In 1870 there was nothing that could be called an American steel industry; by 1900 we were producing more than ten million tons of steel annually—more than all the rest of the world combined.

The economic opportunity in America attracted millions of foreigners to these shores during these decades. These men, women, and children did not uproot themselves from Europe, leaving family and friends, then undertake an uncomfortable ocean voyage, in order to be exploited; they came here because they could, by their own efforts, forge a better life for themselves in the freest economy the world had yet known.

An Economy of Opportunity

The economy was not wholly free, else there would not have been a single robber baron. But the fact that certain sharp operators piled up large fortunes by means of legally sanctioned thievery means that there was already wealth here to be stolen. The wealth they filched from the taxpayers was created by millions of industrious Americans laboring under conditions that approximated the free market. Compared to working conditions in Europe, we had an economy of opportunity. Thirty million immigrants told us so by coming to these shores, where they found a better and freer life for themselves and their descendants.

Let me retrace our steps to the place where I alleged that Gustavus Myers was long on indignation, but somewhat short on theory. He tells the sordid tale of a gang of private citizens in cahoots with government to operate a scam against the public. His fortune hunters are supposed to represent "free enterprise," but in reality, the robber barons are to the market economy what Jesse James and the Dalton brothers were to the hardy homesteaders who settled the western territories. In other words, they were more predators than producers.

We need to come to some understanding of the political order appropriate to a society of free people. By the same token, we need to know how the free economy operates, and the role of the businessman within a market economy.

Politically, I call myself an old-fashioned Whig. I'm a believer in equal justice under the law, and am something of a Jeffersonian, so let me quote a few lines from Jefferson's First Inaugural Address describing the society he strove for: "Equal and exact justice to all men, of whatever state or persuasion, religious or political; peace, commerce, and honest friendships with all nations, entangling alliances with none . . . freedom of religion, and freedom of the press, and freedom of person under the protection of the habeas corpus."

Earlier in the same address Jefferson had praised "a wise and frugal Government, which shall restrain men from injuring one another, shall leave them otherwise free to regulate their own pursuits of industry and improvement, and shall not take from the mouth of labor the bread it has earned."

The function of government, in the Jeffersonian scheme, is to secure the God-given rights of all persons, to deter and redress injury, and otherwise let people alone.

Limited Government

The American Constitution is more explicit in what it forbids government to do than in what it authorizes government to do; the words "no" and "not" in restraint of governmental power occur forty-five times in the first seven Articles and the Bill of Rights. Limiting the scope and power of government maximizes individual liberty and gives us a society of free people. Government, in a free society, has no power to confer economic advantage on some at the expense of others, which eliminates "robber barons," be they individuals or groups, rich or poor. The government of a free people does not misuse its power to tax by taking wealth from those whose labor produced it and allocating it to the pressure groups who possess political influence.

Limited government under the Rule of Law maintains an even-handed justice; it keeps the peace of the community by curbing those who break the peace. It lets people alone, and it punishes any individual who refuses to let other people alone.

A free government is distinguished from other forms of government by the use it makes of the law; it employs lawful force against criminals in order that peaceful people may go about their business. This is force used in self-defense. Every other political system uses legal violence against peaceful people for any sort of reason the users of violence may conjure up. This is the aggressive use of force. The distinction is between law and tyranny, as the Greeks put it. "Let no man live uncurbed by law; nor curbed by tyranny," said the playwright Aeschylus.

Given the law order of a free society, the economic activities of men and women, as they go about the business of earning a livelihood, is necessarily free market and voluntary.

Consumer Sovereignty and the Free Society

In a genuinely free society, a laissez-faire society in the early sense of this much abused phrase, the businessman is a mandatary of consumers; the customer is boss. Consumer sovereignty! Is this the way the businessman likes it? Of course not. Our businessman would like to think of himself as the man in charge, a captain of industry running a tight ship. But who's he kidding? He doesn't even have the power to set wages and prices. His competition, his employees, and his customers make those decisions for him. If he tries to lower wages he will lose his best workers to his competitors who pay the going rate or more. If he tries to raise prices, people buy elsewhere. He's stymied, and that's why he's tempted on occasion to persuade some politician to bend the rules in his favor, just enough to give him what a friend of mine called, ironically, a "fair advantage."

But when a businessman yields to this temptation he forfeits his standing as a businessman and becomes something else—a branch of the government bureaucracy. He has left the economic order, and is now part of the State. As a businessman he had no power over anyone; as a part of the State he shares, with government, the power to tax. People now have to pay for his products whether they buy them or not.

Was there "free enterprise" during the Gilded Age? Yes, there was—but not much of it on the part of the "robber barons" who were in cahoots with government. Was there "individualism" during the period? Well, there was individuality, but the kind of individualism which means equal freedom for every person to pursue his private goals was not a guiding policy.

But who are we, as we go stumbling down the road to serfdom, to cast the first stone?

Witch-Hunting for Robber Barons

by Lawrence W. Reed

Among the great misconceptions of the free economy is the widely held belief that "laissez faire" embodies a natural tendency toward monopoly concentration. Under unfettered capitalism, so goes the familiar refrain, large firms would systematically devour smaller ones, corner markets, and stamp out competition until every inhabitant of the land fell victim to their power. Just as popular is the notion that John D. Rockefeller's Standard Oil Company of the late 1800s gave substance to such an evil course of events.

Regarding Standard Oil's chief executive, one noted historian writes, "He [Rockefeller] ironhandedly ruined competitors by cutting prices until his victim went bankrupt or sold out, whereupon higher prices would be likely to return."[1]

Two other historians, co-authors of a popular college text, opine that "Rockefeller was a ruthless operator who did not hesitate to crush his competitors by harsh and unfair methods."[2]

In 1899, Standard refined 90 percent of America's oil—the peak of the company's dominance of the refining business. Though that market share was steadily siphoned off by competitors after 1899, the company nonetheless has been branded ever since as "an industrial octopus."

Does the story of Standard Oil really present a case *against* the free market? In my opinion, it most emphatically does not. Furthermore, setting the record straight on this issue must become an important weapon in every free market advocate's intellectual arsenal. That's the purpose of the following remarks.

Theoretically, there are two kinds of monopolies: coercive and efficiency. A coercive monopoly results from, in the words of Adam Smith, "a government grant of exclusive privilege." Government, in

---

Mr. Reed is President of the Mackinac Center for Public Policy in Midland, Michigan. This article first appeared in *The Freeman*, March 1980.

effect, must take sides in the market in order to give birth to a coercive monopoly. It must make it difficult, costly, or impossible for anyone but the favored firm to do business.

The United States Postal Service is an example of this kind of monopoly. By law, no one can deliver first-class mail except the USPS. Fines and imprisonment (coercion) await all those daring enough to compete.

In some other cases, the government may not ban competition outright, but simply bestow privileges, immunities, or subsidies on one firm while imposing costly requirements on all others. Regardless of the method, a firm which enjoys a coercive monopoly is in a position to harm the consumer and get away with it.

An efficiency monopoly, on the other hand, earns a high share of a market because it does the best job. It receives no special favors from the law to account for its size. Others are free to compete and, if consumers so will it, to grow as big as the monopoly.

An efficiency monopoly has no legal power to compel people to deal with it or to protect itself from the consequences of its unethical practices. It can only attain bigness through its excellence in satisfying customers and by the economy of its operations. An efficiency monopoly which turns its back on the very performance which produced its success would be posting a sign, "COMPETITORS WANTED." The market rewards excellence and exacts a toll on mediocrity.

It is my contention that the historical record casts the Standard Oil Company in the role of efficiency monopoly—a firm to which consumers repeatedly awarded their votes of confidence.

The oil rush began with the discovery of oil by Colonel Edwin Drake at Titusville, Pennsylvania, in 1859. Northwestern Pennsylvania soon "was overrun with businessmen, speculators, misfits, horse dealers, drillers, bankers, and just plain hell-raisers. Dirt-poor farmers leased land at fantastic prices, and rigs began blackening the landscape. Existing towns jammed full overnight with 'strangers,' and new towns appeared almost as quickly."[3]

In the midst of chaos emerged young John D. Rockefeller. An exceptionally hard-working and thrifty man, Rockefeller transformed his early interest in oil into a partnership in the refinery stage of the business in 1865.

Five years later, Rockefeller formed the Standard Oil Company with 4 percent of the refining market. Less than thirty years later, he

John D. Rockefeller
(1839–1937)

reached that all-time high of 90 percent. What accounts for such stunning success?

On December 30, 1899, Rockefeller was asked that very question before a governmental investigating body called the Industrial Commission. He replied:

> I ascribe the success of the Standard to its consistent policy to make the volume of its business large through the merits and cheapness of its products. It has spared no expense in finding, securing, and utilizing the best and cheapest methods of manufacture. It has sought for the best superintendents and workmen and paid the best wages. It has not hesitated to sacrifice old machinery and old plants for new and better ones. It has placed its manufactories at the points where they could supply markets at the least expense. It has not only sought markets for its principal products, but for all possible by-products,

> sparing no expense in introducing them to the public. It has not hesitated to invest millions of dollars in methods of cheapening the gathering and distribution of oils by pipe lines, special cars, tank steamers, and tank wagons. It has erected tank stations at every important railroad station to cheapen the storage and delivery of its products. It has spared no expense in forcing its products into the markets of the world among people civilized and uncivilized. It has had faith in American oil, and has brought together millions of money for the purpose of making it what it is, and holding its markets against the competition of Russia and all the many countries which are producers of oil and competitors against American oil.[4]

A Master Organizer of Men and Materials

Rockefeller was a managerial genius—a master organizer of men as well as of materials. He had a gift for bringing devoted, brilliant, and hard-working young men into his organization. Among his most outstanding associates were H. H. Rogers, John D. Archbold, Stephen V. Harkness, Samuel Andrews, and Henry M. Flagler. Together they emphasized efficient economic operation, research, and sound financial practices. The economic excellence of their performance is described by economist D. T. Armentano:

> Instead of buying oil from jobbers, they made the jobbers' profit by sending their own purchasing men into the oil region. In addition, they made their own sulfuric acid, their own barrels, their own lumber, their own wagons, and their own glue. They kept minute and accurate records of every item from rivets to barrel bungs. They built elaborate storage facilities near their refineries. Rockefeller bargained as shrewdly for crude as anyone before or since. And Sam Andrews coaxed more kerosene from a barrel of crude than could the competition. In addition, the Rockefeller firm put out the cleanest-burning kerosene, and managed to dispose of most of the residues like lubricating oil, paraffin, and vaseline at a profit.[5]

Even muckraker Ida Tarbell, one of Standard's critics, admired the company's streamlined processes of production:

> Not far away from the canning works, on Newton Creek, is an oil refinery. This oil runs to the canning works, and, as the new-made cans come down by a chute from the works above, where they have just been finished, they are filled, twelve at a time, with the oil made a few miles away. The apparatus is admirable. As the new-made cans come down the chute they are distributed, twelve in a row, along one side of a turn-table. The turn-table is revolved, and the cans come directly under twelve measures, each holding five gallons of oil—a turn of a valve, and the cans are full. The table is turned a quarter, and while twelve more cans are filled and twelve fresh ones are distributed, four men with soldering cappers put the caps on the first set. Another quarter turn, and men stand ready to take the cans from the filler and while they do this, twelve more are having caps put on, twelve are filling, and twelve are coming to their place from the chute. The cans are placed at once in wooden boxes standing ready, and, after a twenty-four-hour wait for discovering leaks, are nailed up and carted to a nearby door. This door opens on the river, and there at anchor by the side of the factory is a vessel chartered for South America or China or where not—waiting to receive the cans which a little more than twenty-four hours before were tin sheets lying on flatboxes. It is a marvelous example of economy, not only in materials, but in time and in footsteps.[6]

Market Competition Protects the Public

Socialist historian Gabriel Kolko, who argues in *The Triumph of Conservatism* that the forces of competition in the free market of the late 1800s were too potent to allow Standard to cheat the public, stresses that "Standard treated the consumer with deference. Crude and refined oil prices for consumers declined during the period Standard exercised greatest control of the industry. . . ."[7]

Standard's service to the consumer in the form of lower prices is well-documented. To quote from Professor Armentano again: "Between 1870 and 1885 the price of refined kerosene dropped from 26 cents to 8 cents per gallon. In the same period, the Standard Oil Company reduced the [refining] costs per gallon from almost 3 cents in 1870 to .452 cents in 1885. Clearly, the firm was relatively efficient, and its efficiency was being translated to the consumer in the form of lower prices for a much improved product, and to the firm in the form of additional profits."[8]

That story continued for the remainder of the century, with the price of kerosene to the consumer falling to 5.91 cents per gallon in 1897. Armentano concludes from the record that "at the very pinnacle of Standard's industry 'control,' *the costs and the prices for refined oil reached their lowest levels in the history of the petroleum industry*."[9]

John D. Rockefeller's success, then, was a consequence of his superior performance. He derived his impressive market share not from government favors but rather from aggressive courting of the consumer. Standard Oil is one of history's classic efficiency monopolies.

But what about the many serious charges leveled against Standard? Predatory price-cutting? Buying out competitors? Conspiracy? Railroad rebates? Charging any price it wanted? Greed? Each of these can be viewed as an assault not just on Standard Oil but on the free market in general. They can and must be answered.

Predatory Price-Cutting

Predatory price-cutting is "the practice of deliberately underselling rivals in certain markets to drive them out of business, and then raising prices to exploit a market devoid of competition."[10]

Professor John S. McGee, writing in the *Journal of Law and Economics* for October 1958, stripped this charge of any intellectual substance. Describing it as "logically deficient," he concluded, "I can find little or no evidence to support it."[11]

In his extraordinary article, McGee scrutinized the testimony of Rockefeller's competitors who claimed to have been victims of predatory price-cutting. He found their claims to be shallow and misdirected. McGee pointed out that some of these very people later opened new refineries and successfully challenged Standard again.

Beyond the actual record, economic theory also argues against a winning policy of predatory price-cutting in a free market for the following reasons:

1. *Price is only one aspect of competition.* Firms compete in a variety of ways: service, location, packaging, marketing, even courtesy. For price alone to draw customers away from the competition, the preda-

tor would have to cut substantially—enough to outweigh all the other competitive pressures the others can throw at him. That means suffering losses on every unit sold. If the predator has a war-chest of "monopoly profits" to draw upon in such a battle, then the predatory price-cutting theorist must explain how he was able to achieve such ability in the absence of this practice in the first place!

2. *The large firm stands to lose the most.* By definition, the large firm is already selling the most units. As a predator, it must actually step up its production if it is to have any effect on competitors. As Professor McGee observed, "To lure customers away from somebody he [the predator] must be prepared to serve them himself. The monopolizer thus finds himself in the position of selling more—and therefore losing more—than his competitors."[12]

3. *Consumers will increase their purchases at the "bargain prices."* This factor causes the predator to step up production even further. It also puts off the day when he can "cash in" on his hoped-for victory because consumers will be in a position to refrain from purchasing at higher prices, consuming their stockpiles instead.

4. *The length of the battle is always uncertain.* The predator does not know how long he must suffer losses before his competitors quit. It may take weeks, months, or even years. Meanwhile, consumers are "cleaning up" at his expense.

5. *Any "beaten" firms may reopen.* Competitors may scale down production or close only temporarily as they "wait out the storm." When the predator raises prices, they enter the market again. Conceivably, a "beaten" firm might be bought up by someone for a "song," and then, under fresh management and with relatively low capital costs, face the predator with an actual competitive cost advantage.

6. *High prices encourage newcomers.* Even if the predator drives everyone else from the market, raising prices will attract competition from people heretofore not even in the industry. The higher the prices go, the more powerful that attraction.

7. *The predator would lose the favor of consumers.* Predatory price-cutting is simply not good public relations. Once known, it would swiftly erode the public's faith and good will. It might even evoke consumer boycotts and a backlash of sympathy for the firm's competitors.

In summary, let me quote Professor McGee once again:

> Judging from the Record, Standard Oil did not use predatory price discrimination to drive out competing refiners, nor did its pricing practice have that effect. Whereas there may be a very few cases in which retail kerosene peddlers or dealers went out of business after or during price-cutting, there is no real proof that Standard's pricing policies were responsible. I am convinced that Standard did not systematically, if ever, use local price-cutting in retailing, or anywhere else, to reduce competition. To do so would have been foolish; and, whatever else has been said about them, the old Standard organization was seldom criticized for making less money when it could readily have made more.[13]

Buying Out Competitors

The intent of this practice, the critics say, was to stifle competitors by absorbing them.

First, it must be said that Standard had no legal power to coerce a competitor into selling. For a purchase to occur, Rockefeller had to pay the *market* price for an oil refinery. And evidence abounds that he often hired the very people whose operations he purchased. "Victimized ex-rivals," wrote McGee, "might be expected to make poor employees and dissident or unwilling shareholders."[14]

Kolko writes that "Standard attained its control of the refinery business primarily by mergers, not price wars, and most refinery owners were anxious to sell out to it. Some of these refinery owners later reopened new plants after selling to Standard."[15]

Buying out competitors can be a wise move if achieving economy of scale is the intent. Buying out competitors merely to eliminate them from the market can be a futile, expensive, and never-ending policy. It appears that Rockefeller's mergers were designed with the first motive in mind.

Even so, other people found it profitable to go into the business of building refineries and selling to Standard. David P. Reighard managed to build and sell three successive refineries to Rockefeller, all on excellent terms.

A firm which adopts a policy of absorbing others solely to stifle competition embarks upon the impossible adventure of putting out the recurring and unpredictable prairie fires of competition.

Conspiracy to Fix Prices

This accusation holds that Standard secured secret agreements with competitors to carve up markets and fix prices at higher-than-market levels.

I will not contend here that Rockefeller never attempted this policy. His experiment with the South Improvement Company in 1872 provides at least some evidence that he did. I do argue, however, that all such attempts were failures from the start and no harm to the consumer occurred.

Standard's price performance, cited extensively above, supports my argument. Prices fell steadily on an improving product. Some conspiracy!

From the perspective of economic theory, collusion to raise and/or fix prices is a practice doomed to failure in a free market for these reasons:

1. *Internal pressures*. Conspiring firms must resolve the dilemma of production. To exact a higher price than the market currently permits, production must be curtailed. Otherwise, in the face of a fall in demand, the firms will be stuck with a quantity of unsold goods. Who will cut their production and by how much? Will the conspirators accept an equal reduction for all when it is likely that each faces a unique constellation of cost and distribution advantages and disadvantages?

Assuming a formula for restricting production is agreed upon, it then becomes highly profitable for any member of the cartel to quietly cheat on the agreement. By offering secret rebates or discounts or other "deals" to his competitors' customers, any conspirator can undercut the cartel price, earn an increasing share of the market and make a lot of money. When the others get wind of this, they must quickly break the agreement or lose their market shares to the "cheater." The very reason for the conspiracy in the first place—higher profits—proves to be its undoing!

2. *External pressures*. This comes from competitors who are not parties to the secret agreement. They feel under no obligation to abide by the cartel price and actually use their somewhat lower price as a selling point to customers. The higher the cartel price, the more this external competition pays. The conspiracy must either convince all outsiders to join the cartel (making it increasingly likely that somebody will cheat) or else dissolve the cartel to meet the competition.

I would once again call the reader's attention to Kolko's *The Triumph of Conservatism,* which documents the tendency for collusive agreements to break apart, sometimes even before the ink is dry.

Railroad Rebates

John D. Rockefeller received substantial rebates from railroads who hauled his oil, a factor which critics claim gave him an unfair advantage over other refiners.

The fact is that most all refiners received rebates from railroads. This practice was simply evidence of stiff competition among the roads for the business of hauling refined oil products. Standard got the biggest rebates because Rockefeller was a shrewd bargainer and because he offered the railroads large volume on a regular basis.

This charge is even less credible when one considers that Rockefeller increasingly relied on his own pipelines, not railroads, to transport his oil.

The Power to Charge Any Price Wanted

According to the notion that Standard's size gave it the power to charge any price it wanted, bigness per se immunizes the firm from competition and consumer sovereignty.

As an "efficiency monopoly," Standard could not coercively prevent others from competing with it. And others did, so much so that the company's share of the market declined dramatically after 1899. As the economy shifted from kerosene to electricity, from the horse to the automobile, and from oil production in the East to production in the Gulf States, Rockefeller found himself losing ground to younger, more aggressive men.

Neither did Standard have the power to compel people to buy its products. It had to rely on its own excellence to attract and keep customers.

In a totally free market, the following factors insure that no firm, regardless of size, can charge and get "any price it wants":

1. *Free entry.* Potential competition is encouraged by any firm's abuse of the consumer. In describing entry into the oil business, Rockefeller once remarked that "all sorts of people . . . the butcher, the baker, and the candlestick maker began to refine oil."[16]

2. *Foreign competition.* As long as government doesn't hamper international trade, this is always a potent force.

3. *Competition of substitutes.* People are often able to substitute a product different from yet similar to the monopolist's.

4. *Competition of all goods for the consumer's dollar.* Every businessman is in competition with every other businessman to get consumers to spend their limited dollars on him.

5. *Elasticity of demand.* At higher prices, people will simply buy less.

It makes sense to view competition in a free market not as a static phenomenon, but as a dynamic, never-ending, leap-frog process by which the leader today can be the follower tomorrow.

Rockefeller Was Greedy

The charge that John D. Rockefeller was a "greedy" man is the most meaningless of all the attacks on him but nonetheless echoes constantly in the history books.

If Rockefeller wanted to make a lot of money (and there is no doubting he did), he certainly discovered the free market solution to his problem: produce and sell something that consumers will buy and buy again. One of the great attributes of the free market is that it channels greed into constructive directions. One cannot accumulate wealth without offering something in exchange!

At this point the reader might rightly wonder about the dissolution of the Standard Oil Trust in 1911. Didn't the Supreme Court find Standard guilty of successfully employing anti-competitive practices?

Interestingly, a careful reading of the decision reveals that no attempt was made by the Court to examine Standard's conduct or performance. The justices did not sift through the conflicting evidence concerning any of the government's allegations against the company. No specific finding of guilt was made with regard to those charges. Although the record clearly indicates that "prices fell, costs fell, outputs expanded, product quality improved, and hundreds of firms at one time or another produced and sold refined petroleum products in competition with Standard Oil,"[17] the Supreme Court ruled against the company. The justices argued simply that the competition between some of the divisions of Standard Oil was less than the competition that existed between them when they were separate companies before merging with Standard.

In 1915, Charles W. Eliot, president of Harvard, observed: "The organization of the great business of taking petroleum out of the earth, piping the oil over great distances, distilling and refining it, and distributing it in tank steamers, tank wagons, and cans all over the earth, was an American invention."[18] Let the facts record that the great Standard Oil Company, more than any other firm, and John D. Rockefeller, more than any other man, were responsible for this amazing development.

---

1. Thomas A. Bailey, *The American Pageant: A History of the Republic,* 2 vols., 3rd ed. (Boston: D. C. Heath and Company, 1966), II, p. 532.
2. Gilbert C. Fite and Jim E. Reese, *An Economic History of the United States,* 2nd ed. (Boston: Houghton Mifflin Company, 1965), p. 367.
3. D. T. Armentano, *The Myths of Antitrust: Economic Theory and Legal Cases* (New Rochelle, N.Y.: Arlington House, 1972), p. 64.
4. Thomas G. Manning, E. David Cronon, and Howard R. Lamar, *The Standard Oil Company: The Rise of a National Monopoly, Government and the American Economy: 1870 to the Present,* (New York: Henry Holt and Company, 1960), p. 19.
5. Armentano, *Myths of Antitrust,* p. 67.
6. Ida M. Tarbell, *The History of the Standard Oil Company,* 2 vols. in 1 (Gloucester, Mass.: Peter Smith, 1950), pp. 240–241.
7. Gabriel Kolko, *The Triumph of Conservatism: A Reinterpretation of American History, 1900–1916* (New York: The Macmillan Company, 1963; reprint ed., Chicago: Quadrangle Books, 1967), p. 39.
8. Armentano, *Myths of Antitrust,* p. 70.
9. *Ibid.,* p. 77.
10. *Ibid.,* p. 73.
11. John S. McGee, "Predatory Price-cutting: The Standard Oil (N.J.) Case," *Journal of Law and Economics,* October 1958, p. 138.
12. *Ibid.,* p. 140.
13. *Ibid.,* p. 168.
14. *Ibid.,* p. 145.
15. Kolko, *Triumph of Conservatism,* p. 40.
16. John A. Garraty, *The American Nation: A History of the United States Since 1865,* 3rd ed. (New York: Harper and Row 1975), II, p. 499.
17. Armentano, *Myths of Antitrust,* p. 83.
18. Fite and Reese, *An Economic History,* p. 366.

John Arbuckle: Entrepreneur, Trust Buster, Humanitarian

by Clayton A. Coppin

The importance of the entrepreneur to the spectacular growth of the American economy in the late nineteenth and early twentieth centuries is now widely understood. The contributions of John D. Rockefeller, Andrew Carnegie, and J. P. Morgan are well known.

There are other entrepreneurs, however, whose names and achievements are not so familiar. Among the forgotten is John Arbuckle, whose recognition as an outstanding entrepreneur and humanitarian is long overdue. He deserves equal recognition as one who fought against monopolistic practices, and who relied on his own business skills rather than government regulation to compete.

John Arbuckle was born in Allegheny City, Pennsylvania, near Pittsburgh, in 1838. His father, Thomas Arbuckle, immigrated to western Pennsylvania from Scotland as a young man and became the successful operator of a cotton mill and a small grocery and spice business. John attended public school in Allegheny and Pittsburgh, and he attended Washington and Jefferson College for a short time. But formal education held little appeal for him. He was more interested in business, so he dropped out of school to enter the grocery business with his brother Charles.

John and Charles Arbuckle soon expanded into the coffee-roasting business. At the time, coffee was roasted and stored in bulk. The grocer would scoop out the amount desired by the customer and place it in a smaller package. This method had disadvantages—coffee left open in the air after roasting deteriorated rapidly; high quality and low quality were mixed together; it was easy to adulterate; the grocer's scale wasn't always reliable. The Arbuckles found a way to avoid these problems.

Clayton A. Coppin is Research Associate Professor at the Center for the Study of Market Processes, George Mason University, Fairfax, Virginia. This article is reprinted from the May 1990 issue of *The Freeman*. An earlier version of the essay, with full footnote citations, appeared in the spring 1989 issue of *Market Process,* published by the Center for the Study of Market Processes.

They roasted coffee and wrapped it in individual packages of uniform weight and quality. They could sell different grades of coffee at different prices, and guarantee the weight and quality of their brand-name product.

Their business grew quickly, and in 1871 they moved to New York City and formed the Arbuckle Brothers Company. Business continued to expand, and at one point they employed 50 women just to wrap the coffee. John felt that manual wrapping was inefficient and that operating costs were too high. He saw the packaging process as a bottleneck and sought a way to eliminate it. With the aid of a draftsman and a machinist, he invented a machine that would fill, weigh, seal, and label the bags in one continuous operation. Once installed, the machinery increased the production tenfold, doing the work of 500 wrappers.

With the increased production, the Arbuckle brothers expanded their distribution, improved their procurement system in coffee-producing countries, and began an aggressive advertising campaign. They quickly developed a national market and became the dominant coffee company in the United States. Particularly popular was their Ariosa brand, which was a coffee bean glazed with a sugar and egg coating. The egg was supposed to cause a quick settling of the grounds, and the sugar added sweetness to the already high quality of the coffee. Whatever the virtues of Ariosa, the product's reputation for consistency and quality led to further expansion of market share.

Seeking a New Market

Having won much of the coffee market, the brothers sought a new market for expansion. John Arbuckle developed and patented a machine that automatically filled and sealed sugar bags. They made an arrangement with Henry O. Havemeyer, who controlled the American Sugar Trust, to produce sugar in two-pound bags. Once again they found a ready market for their packaged goods, and made substantial inroads in the retail sugar market.

Charles Arbuckle's death in 1890 didn't slow the company's growth, but Henry Havemeyer was soon to try. Havemeyer had become the leading force in the American sugar-refining industry, driving all but a few small companies out of business. Havemeyer realized that if profits were too high it would invite new entrants into the field.

He attempted to avoid this by keeping prices reasonable, by making rebate agreements with the railroads, and by arranging for price maintenance with wholesale grocers.

Havemeyer kept ahead of the competition for several years until a conflict erupted with Arbuckle. What exactly led to the break isn't known. Perhaps Arbuckle wanted a lower price because of his volume buying, or, more likely, Havemeyer, seeing Arbuckle as a growing competitor, raised Arbuckle's price for refined sugar. Whatever the exact cause, Arbuckle announced his intention to build a sugar refinery. Havemeyer had no intention of allowing new competition in the sugar refining business. The resulting battle would become one of the legendary competitive struggles in American business history.

Arbuckle broke ground in Brooklyn in January 1897 for his sugar refinery, but it would be nearly two years before it was producing. Meanwhile Havemeyer decided to retaliate by entering the coffee business. He purchased controlling interest in the Woolson Spice Company in Toledo, Ohio, and immediately started lowering prices. Arbuckle responded and the price quickly dropped until both companies were selling below costs.

The battle was not to be fought on the price front alone. Havemeyer advertised heavily, obtained rebates from railroads, and attempted to keep wholesalers from handling Arbuckle's product. International shipping was dragged into the battle when Havemeyer managed to obtain shipping rebates. Arbuckle responded by buying his own ships. Havemeyer made inroads into the coffee market, but at a very high cost.

Havemeyer was unable to stop Arbuckle from entering the sugar business and, when Arbuckle's refinery started producing in late 1898, the price war extended to sugar. Both companies were now losing money in sugar and coffee. Havemeyer was receiving rebates from the railroads for the sugar he shipped as well as on what Arbuckle shipped, and he attempted to control the wholesalers by threatening to break the price maintenance agreements with them if they carried Arbuckle's sugar.

Havemeyer would seem to have had the advantage in the sugar fight. However, although both companies were selling at a loss, Havemeyer's greater market share led to higher losses. In addition, since Arbuckle alone sold sugar in small packages, he was able to obtain a higher price per unit and suffered smaller losses. Arbuckle challenged

John Arbuckle
(1839–1912)

Havemeyer's control of the wholesalers by selling directly to retailers, and eventually forced the wholesalers to cooperate to avoid being bypassed. Arbuckle gained another advantage by hiring Joseph Stillman, a former employee of Havemeyer and the leading expert on sugar refining in the country. Stillman designed and built Arbuckle's refinery using the latest technology, which produced a superior product at a lower cost.

The End of the War

The battle over sugar couldn't continue indefinitely with the size of the losses both companies were sustaining. No record has been found of a settlement, but sometime in 1901, after Havemeyer and Arbuckle held a private meeting, the price war in sugar ended. Havemeyer accepted Arbuckle's presence in the sugar refining business and made no further attempts to drive him out. To recover from the loss, however, both companies substantially increased their prices, which quickly led to additional entries, most notably by Claus Spreckels. Havemeyer's companies would continue to hold a strong market share, but the days of his domination of the industry were over.

Arbuckle was more clearly the victor in the coffee battle. He had managed to obtain a few shares of the Woolson Spice Company and through a stockholders' suit forced the company to stop selling at a loss. Prior to this, however, an interesting episode emerged during the battle in Ohio. In early 1901, Edward Beverstock, a food and dairy inspector in Toledo, charged a retailer selling Arbuckle's Ariosa coffee with violating Ohio's pure food law. Arbuckle was charged with adulterating his coffee beans by adding the egg and sugar glaze for the purposes of increasing the weight and covering up inferiority. Arbuckle had attempted to meet all requirements of the law, carefully labeling his product and having it analyzed for purity. Who or what was behind the charges isn't known, but the timing and subsequent events suggest Havemeyer might have been involved.

The trial was held in Toledo, and in spite of expert testimony for the defense from scientific witnesses such as Harvey Washington Wiley, Chief Chemist for the U.S. Department of Agriculture and the nation's leading advocate of pure food, the jury found Arbuckle guilty. The appeals court reversed the conviction. They found that the jury had been improperly selected, that individuals closely associated with Inspector Beverstock and his son had been placed in the jury pool, and that the judge had erred in not allowing the defense to challenge the way the jury was selected. The Appellate Court also found that Ariosa coffee wasn't covered by the statutes under which the original complaint had been made. Arbuckle was cleared of all charges. The numerous irregularities in the trial would seem to indicate that more was involved than protecting the consumer in Ohio.

While Arbuckle clearly entered sugar refining for commercial reasons, he objected to organizations which were formed to obtain monopoly profits. He did not, however, believe that government interference was the solution. He preferred to call on his own abilities and finances to challenge monopoly control of a market. His entry into these markets resulted in the breakup of the monopolies without government interference.

The fight with the sugar trust was the most spectacular of Arbuckle's challenges to monopolies, but not the only one. Earlier he had challenged and successfully overthrown the towing monopoly which controlled traffic on the Erie Canal. In 1901, as his fight with Havemeyer wound down, Arbuckle turned his attention to the tugboat monopoly on the Hudson River. Deciding that the rate of $50 for a tow from New York to Albany was excessive, he entered the market. The price of towing quickly dropped, reaching a low of $5. One barge owner reportedly said, "They'll be giving trading stamps next." Another barge owner claimed that he had been offered money to have his boat towed up the river. The final outcome was a permanent lowering of towing costs.

John Arbuckle's fights against trusts demonstrate the power of the entrepreneur to challenge those who would restrict entry into markets. He didn't seek government intervention and regulation of the market. There is a great difference between an entrepreneur who breaks up a trust by open competition, and a businessman who tries to hamper his competitors by complaining to the Department of Justice or the Federal Trade Commission. The entrepreneur provides a public service by improving a product or lowering prices. The complainer usually hampers the efficiency of those he cannot compete with in the open market. Today, over two-thirds of antitrust cases in the United States are initiated by competitors who cannot meet the superior efficiency of their rivals. Far better that they would follow the example of Arbuckle, who used his inventive, organizational, and commercial abilities to challenge those who wanted to limit competition.

Arbuckle as Philanthropist

However, there was more to John Arbuckle than just his business accomplishments. He also had a remarkable record as a humanitarian. For many years in Brooklyn he was a member of the congregation of the Plymouth Church headed by Henry Ward Beecher, the noted reformer and the brother of Harriet Beecher Stowe. He shared Beecher's concern for his fellow men, and he brought to his humanitarian concerns the same genius he displayed in his commercial activities.

Arbuckle's inventiveness involved him in several efforts to help New York City's needy. Convinced that overcrowding, bad air, and the hustle and bustle of city life were bad for health, he financed several projects to help people escape from city life. The most fanciful of these was the outfitting of several ships with rooms, recreational facilities, and dining rooms, then towing them out to sea at night. The plan was to give people who couldn't otherwise afford to escape from city life the benefits of fresh ocean breezes and a sound diet. The scheme was short lived, but the ships, tied to the docks, continued to be used for charitable purposes providing shelter, low-cost meals, and job training sites to the needy for many years. One boat was converted into the Riverside Home for Crippled Children.

On Lake Mohonk north of New York City he built a retirement colony for older citizens who needed assistance, and a hotel for those who needed fresh air and nutritious food. He also built hotels for workers who needed to be out in the open, and hotels for the handicapped to learn a trade. Arbuckle seldom gave to established charities, preferring to experiment with his own ideas.

As a result of the Ariosa coffee case, Arbuckle became a friend of Harvey W. Wiley and developed an interest in the pure food movement. His interest, however, was not to support regulation, but to try to establish a company to produce pure and nutritious food with Wiley as the company's head. Arbuckle several times made offers to Wiley to finance the business, but Wiley never took up the offer. On Wiley's suggestion, Arbuckle did establish an independent sugar-testing laboratory to monitor the quality of sugar in the American market.

Arbuckle, even in his old age, was interested in new and inventive ideas and willing to take on new ventures. Following the end of his fight with Havemeyer, Arbuckle became interested in the ship-salvage business. He was attracted to the work of two Canadians, R. O. King and William Wotherspoon, who developed a method for using compressed air to refloat ships. He contacted them and began salvaging ships that others had regarded as impossible to refloat. He offered to go to Havana Harbor and raise the battleship *Maine,* but his offer was refused. He wanted the government to establish a warning system so that a ship in distress could call for help and salvage vessels could rush to its aid, but the government wasn't interested. Arbuckle proceeded to establish his own system and rescued several ships.

Arbuckle later spoke out strongly against the duties on sugar, arguing that the duties were only for the benefit of the sugar beet interests and at the expense of all other Americans. He pointed out that sugar was used by the rich and poor alike, and the added expense was felt most by the poor. To charge duties on sugar, Arbuckle argued, was a case of the government literally taking candy from babies. In 1911 he announced his intention to fight the duties as soon as his health improved. He had for many years suffered from malaria, which frequently incapacitated him. His condition deteriorated, and on March 27, 1912, he died. With better health, however, he might have left an even more remarkable record.

This article has explored some of the contributions John Arbuckle made to building the American economy. His innovations in packaging and marketing coffee and sugar marked a significant change in the retail food market. This was more than a simple technological improvement; it was a reordering of the market. It changed not only the production process, but also the way the product was distributed and sold.

The Power of the Entrepreneur

Arbuckle's competitive struggles with the established market system also demonstrate how the entrepreneur can change the existing order. Henry O. Havemeyer, through his American Sugar Trust, was able to control competition in the older order, but he lost to Arbuckle because of the innovations Arbuckle brought to the competition. The career of John Arbuckle is more than the story of an entrepreneur; it is a demonstration of the process of change in the market caused by entrepreneurship.

Arbuckle's humanitarian endeavors contained the same type of innovative activity as his commercial enterprises. Little attention is paid to the importance of the entrepreneur in providing humanitarian services. It is assumed that the entrepreneur is motivated by personal gain, and, therefore, the entrepreneurial process is not important in providing humanitarian services. Arbuckle's efforts would suggest that improvements in humanitarian services can benefit from the entrepreneurial process. It may well be that improvements in humanitarian activities require the same type of innovativeness and new combinations for improved efficiency that economic growth requires.

A Lesson in Time

by John O. Nelson

A veritable frenzy to multiply government regulation presently rules almost every electorate and every legislature. What are we to say of this obsession? We might point out that it has a close affinity to the practices of socialism. But is it, therefore, wrong? May it not be justified? Is not law a good, something we all desire? Let us examine the last question first.

We do not desire our own oppression. That can be affirmed with certainty. Do government laws oppress us? And if so, all laws, or only some? The answer is: some do, and some do not.

Some government laws prohibit what we find it no effort not to do and command what we find it no effort to do. There are, for instance, laws against murder and laws that command us to drive on the right-hand side of the street.

These and like laws are not oppressive nor do we find them to be. But plainly, many laws that are legislated by government do exact from us an effort in our obeying them. The farmer, for example, has to curtail or ignore his own judgment and desires in obeying laws that tell him just how much he may plant. That takes effort. And so does having to measure his acreage, having to fill out the many forms that always accompany such laws, and so on. When a law exacts effort from us it is, to that extent, oppressive. Thus, we may conclude that most current government regulation is oppressive. Moreover, even laws that taken separately might not be oppressive become oppressive when multiplied sufficiently. It does not require any particular effort, for instance, to drive on the right-hand side of the street; but if this regulation is combined with a hundred others as innocuous, just keeping in mind what all the regulations are and attempting to obey them all requires effort. Thus, we find oppressive the mere number of laws and regulations.

Dr. Nelson is Professor Emeritus of Philosophy at the University of Colorado. His articles and papers have appeared in numerous scholarly journals and books in the United States and abroad. This article is reprinted from *The Freeman,* May 1968.

What justification is offered, then, for this present insistence on multiplying laws? A typical excuse is that without government regulation men's lives and affairs must lapse into chaos. This prevalent belief makes it seem incumbent that every nook and cranny of our lives and affairs be regulated by government, no matter how oppressive such regulation may be; for nothing, we shall be inclined to admit, is worse than chaos. I take exception to the belief that without government regulation men's affairs and lives must lapse into chaos. How, though, can the validity of my view be demonstrated?

If we could cite a case where order in a certain area of men's affairs prevailed without government regulation, we should have gone a long way in substantiating our claim. But, even more conclusive would be to cite a case where government actually opposed private efforts to produce order out of chaos and, yet, order was produced. For this case would be tantamount in kind to what is sometimes called a "crucial experiment" in science. All important variables would be accounted for and controlled: a certain chaotic condition in man's affairs; private effort; and government action. A determinate result would be obtained through the direct agency of private effort—namely, order where there had been chaos. Since government action was moving in an opposite direction to private action with respect to the result obtained, it could not be held that government action was somehow *indirectly* the cause of this result. Thus, private effort must have been the cause; and hence, government regulation could not be claimed to be the necessary condition of order in men's affairs.

A Time to Remember

Let us envisage, first, the possible case of every city and general locality in the United States having its own time, determined by the position of the sun at noon. And let us compound this variety of times by supposing that a vast network of railroads exists and that each railroad employs the time of its home terminal in all its operations and schedules. In picturing this state of affairs, we picture—I think it must be agreed—a temporal chaos. We may suppose, moreover, that this chaotic multiplicity of times would impose almost unsupportable burdens on travelers, shippers, and the railroads. Presumably, we have been envisaging a mere possibility. Has any such state of temporal chaos ever in fact existed in the United States? A look at history reveals that it has.

Before 1883, local time—that is, time determined by the local noonday position of the sun—prevailed throughout the United States. Thus, there were more than 26 local times in Michigan, 38 in Wisconsin, 27 in Illinois, and 23 in Indiana. A traveler going by rail from Maine to California had to change his watch 20 times during the trip if he meant to keep accurate time. In addition, each railroad operated its trains according to the local time of its home terminal. The Pennsylvania Railroad, whose home terminal was in Philadelphia, employed a time that was five minutes slower, for example, than New York's, the home terminal of the New York Central, and five minutes faster than Baltimore's, the home terminal of the Baltimore & Ohio. Not surprisingly, this multiplicity of time standards confounded passengers, shippers, and railway employees alike. Errors in keeping time and correlating local times resulted in innumerable inconveniences and costly disasters. Passengers missed trains in wholesale lots; the trains themselves frequently collided.[1]

The Time-Table Convention

Something obviously had to be done. Given our contemporary prejudices, we would naturally think that government had to step in and did step in to bring order out of chaos by legislating the time zones with which we are familiar today. But not so at all.

What actually happened was poles apart. By 1872, a majority of railroad executives were convinced that some system of time zones should be established. A meeting of railroad superintendents was convoked in St. Louis, calling itself initially the Time-Table Convention and later the General Time Convention. Under the guidance of its secretary, William Allen, former resident engineer of the Camden & Amboy Railroad, plans were drawn up to eliminate the chaotic multiplicity of local times. The first plans projected the adoption of time zones bounded by meridians an even hour apart. None of these plans passed the muster of close examination. Finally, in 1881, Allen conceived the idea of five time zones based, not on theoretical considerations, but practical knowledge of geography, economics, the location of large cities, and the general habits of the populace. The plan provided for time zones roughly divided at the 75th, 90th, 105th, and 120th meridians west of Greenwich and thus falling approximately on the longitudes of Philadelphia, Memphis, Denver, and Fresno. The General Time Convention adopted Allen's plan on October 11, 1883, and selected the noon of November 18 as the moment it should go into effect. At that precise moment the railroads, all acting in perfect concert, changed their operations and schedules from local to the new time.[2]

Let us note: this regulation of time initiated by the railroads was a purely private undertaking. The new time zones had no force of law. No one except railroad employees was compelled to set his watch by the new standards. What, then, was the response of the general public? A few preachers thundered that the change of time "was a lie" and "un-Christian," a few newspaper editors objected that the railroads were tyrannically dictating time to 55,000,000 Americans and should be stopped by law from doing so, and some local politicians cried that the act was "unconstitutional, being an attempt to change the immutable laws of God Almighty and hard on the workingman by changing day into night."[3] Despite these isolated fulminations, the general public found the change good and adopted it. Without being forced, people by and large set their watches by the new railroad time; towns and cities followed—indeed, had to follow—suit.

Government's Role

Now, all this time, what was the attitude or response of government? As we have already noted, some local governments and their officials opposed the new dispensation, though the opposition proved ineffective. What about the federal government? Surely—behind the scenes at least—it must have loaned a helping hand to the Time-Table Convention and encouraged or indeed inspired the bringing of order out of chaos! But, again, not so. In fact, the very opposite. Let me quote from H. Stewart Holbrook's illuminating account:

> The traveling public, and shipper too, quickly fell in with the new timebelt plan, and naturally found it good. But Uncle Sam wasn't ready to admit the change was beneficial. A few days before November 18th the Attorney General of the

> United States issued an order that no government department had a right to adopt railroad time until authorized by Congress. The railroads went right ahead with the plan, and the Attorney General, according to a good but perhaps apocryphal story, went to the Washington depot late in the afternoon of the 18th to take a train for Philadelphia. He was greatly astonished, it was reported, to find he was exactly 8 minutes and 20 seconds too late.[4]

It might be added that on March 19, 1918—a full generation after the general adoption of railroad time by the country—Congress passed the Standard Time Act, which gave (to what purpose, it is hard to see) a government commission power to define by law the boundaries of each time zone. One is reminded here of a plagiarist who, having stolen and in the process mangled another man's work, then takes credit for its creation.

Correcting a Misconception

We have demonstrated as conclusively as such things can be demonstrated that government regulation is not necessary to the existence of order in men's lives and affairs. The belief that it is, therefore, is false. Does it follow that we have shown that the current multiplication of oppressive government regulation is unjustified? Not quite. We have shown that this current practice is not justified by the belief that without government regulation men's affairs would lapse into chaos.

It might be claimed, however, that the present multiplication of oppressive law can be justified on other assumptions. For example, it might be argued that though private effort as well as government regulation can produce order in men's affairs, government regulation can produce greater order, or greater safety, or greater security, or greater prosperity; and that, on these grounds, the multiplicity of government regulation currently taking place is justified, even though oppressive. Now, I am sure that each of these claims can be shown to be absolutely false. I merely want to point out that we have not shown this in the present paper. Our results have thus been more limited.

The many-headed monster of socialistic misconception which dominates the modern mind is not likely to be slain by one blow.

However, cutting off one of its heads is a step toward its eventual destruction. We have, I believe, lopped off the most central and voracious one.

---

1. Stewart H. Holbrook, *The Story of American Railroads* (New York: Crown Publishers, 1947), pp. 354–355.

2. *Ibid.*, pp. 355–356.

3. *Ibid.*, pp. 356–357.

4. *Ibid.*, p. 359.

Man at His Best

by Robin Lampson

The willingness of people to help others who are suddenly overwhelmed by a great emergency or disaster is one of the more pleasing characteristics of human beings.

The most amazing instance of this which I can remember occurred right after the great earthquake of April 18, 1906, and the terrible fire in San Francisco that followed. The story I tell here is something I witnessed myself, and I have never come across anything other than the merest generalities about it in books or magazine articles I have read about that holocaust—although the newspapers no doubt reported details of it at the time.

I was a youngster just two-and-a-half months past the age of six that April morning, and nearing the completion of the first grade of grammar school. I woke to find my small bed dancing around the room, with my father holding on to the footboard. I cried out, "What are you pushing my bed around for, Pa?" I didn't realize that he was holding on to my bed so as to stay on his feet during the earthquake!

This was not in San Francisco, but in the small town of Geyserville, in upper Sonoma County, 75 miles north of the metropolis. The temblor did a great deal of damage in that area also, razing many buildings in Santa Rosa and Healdsburg, and leaving hardly a chimney standing in our small town.

Before my father let go of my bed we heard the sound of bricks falling on the roof. "There go the chimneys!" Dad commented forlornly.

It wasn't long before we learned we had lost the brick chimneys of both our kitchen range and living-room stove, and that most of our windows were broken. In addition, my mother lost more than half of her dishes, and she was further saddened because quite a number of cans and glass jars of home-canned fruits and vegetables had been shaken off of shelves and ruined.

This essay appeared in *Pacific Historian,* Fall 1975, and was reprinted with permission in *The Freeman,* March 1988.

My father—the town blacksmith—had to set up a camp stove in the backyard so my mother could cook breakfast. Fortunately, his smithy was at the very north end of the small business section of Geyserville, and his shop and our home and barn, chicken-house, windmill, and water tank were all on a four-or-five acre "lot" that was pretty much like a small farm. We had a couple of cows, a few pigs, 40 or 50 chickens, an acre or so of various grapes, a dozen or more different kinds of fruit trees, several varieties of berry vines, and a vegetable garden that made excellent use of every remaining square foot of available ground.

That April morning ushered in a clear, warm spring day as well as an earthquake for us—and the quake did not disturb the flow of food from our cows and chickens and garden. After breakfast, I hurried downtown with a couple of my older brothers to see what had happened to the dozen or so business places of the village.

Nearly all the front windows of the stores were shattered, and all the glass lay in splinters on the sidewalks. But the real thrill came when we reached the town's lone candy store and soda fountain. The owner, named Elmer Nordyke, stood in the doorway sadly surveying the wreckage.

Inside, the candy showcases were all overturned, and candy was strewn all over the floor, and also out on the sidewalk from the display behind the now completely shattered plate glass front window. "Help yourselves, kids," said Mr. Nordyke, smiling rather sadly. (I hardly need add that no second invitation was necessary.)

Since the daily newspapers immediately stopped coming through from San Francisco, and long-distance telephone service was still in its infancy, the wildest of rumors began circulating. But freight and passenger trains were still running in both directions on the Northwestern Pacific Railroad and the telegraph lines were still open—though in those days in that area the telegraph offices were all in railway stations. But the news which the wires brought to us from Sausalito, across the bay from San Francisco, was only of catastrophe so often told that there is no need for me to repeat it here.

A Desperate Need

A day or so later word began coming through by telegraph that food was desperately needed for the hungry, homeless tens of thousands of quake and fire victims in San Francisco. Then one morning, the daily northbound freight train from Sausalito shunted an empty boxcar onto a siding at the Geyserville depot.

The local depot agent of the Northwestern Pacific lost no time in spreading the appeal which he had received by telegraph. The railroad was leaving one or more empty boxcars at each of its stations along the entire route—and appealed to the people of each community to fill these cars with any food they could spare for San Francisco. The railroad, of course, was contributing the transportation.

The word got around very fast, and the appeal was nothing less than electrifying. Every farmer who came into town heard about it—and took pains to inform his neighbors on the way back home, and neighbors were asked to inform their neighbors farther on. The rural mail carrier, with his horse and buggy, stopping at every roadside mailbox, was also highly effective in spreading the message.

The town or community of Geyserville, with about forty homes around the small business section, in 1906 couldn't have had a total population of more than 400 if one included all the farms within a radius of four or five miles. Yet, within a couple of hours, men, women, and children began coming to that boxcar with baskets and packages and armloads of food.

They brought loaves of homemade bread, mason jars of home-canned fruits and vegetables, sacks of potatoes, bags of dry beans, rice, and sugar, and jars of fresh milk and newly churned butter. As the day wore on, people from the town and nearby farms began bringing in cooked chickens and roasts of beef, veal, pork, and lamb.

This is all the more remarkable when you bear in mind that there was not only no radio or television in those days, but also the telephone and automobile had not yet arrived in our small community. There were a few—very few—bicycles around, but otherwise everyone traveled either by horse or on foot. Yet the appeal kept on spreading fast, for neighbor told neighbor.

Ours was a large family, with nine children, and each year my mother "put up" several hundred quarts of tomatoes, green beans, peas, apricots, cherries, peaches, pears, and berries—in one- and two-quart mason jars or in tin cans sealed on top with wax. In addition, that amazing woman filled scores of glasses and jars of all sizes and shapes with jellies and jams. (In addition to the fruits and vegetables which we grew on our place, my father received various other produce, such as potatoes and pumpkins, squash and melons, raisins and dried prunes and other fruits, also turkeys and sides of veal, pork, and lamb, in exchange for horse-shoeing and other blacksmith work for farmers.)

Now in April 1906, my parents decided to split the remainder of our winter supply of "canned" fruits and vegetables with the hungry people of San Francisco. But what my parents gave was only typical of the donation of practically every household in the community. And the storekeepers of the town also contributed from their shelves and storerooms. In addition, volunteer workers came to the boxcar and helped to pack the food in boxed cartons, and crates; and a couple of carpenters, working with boards and nails donated by the local lumberyard and hardware store, shored up the load inside the car so that the food would ride safely to Sausalito, where it would be ferried to San Francisco.

Before dark the first day the boxcar was nearly full, sealed by the station agent, and ready to roll. And that night the southbound freight train carried the car to its destination.

The next morning the northbound freight left another empty car on the siding—and the amazing spontaneous process of filling it began all over again. And from what I remember hearing at the time, the same sort of response was happening at all the other stations along the railroad.

The day of the earthquake my father immediately made temporary repairs to our kitchen chimney, using stovepipe instead of brick, so that my mother could use our old-fashioned kitchen range. There was no "little old bakeshop" in the town, so housewives did all their own baking. That evening my mother did what many other housewives in the town were doing: she made up several large washpans full of fragrantly yeasty bread dough, which she "set to rise" overnight.

The next morning before dawn my father lit a good fire in the range, and soon my mother had two large bread pans, each with six large loaves, baking and filling the kitchen with their mouth-watering aroma. When these loaves came out of the oven, my mother laid them out to cool under clean white flour sacks made into dish towels—and immediately put another batch of 12 loaves into the oven.

That afternoon she wrapped each panful of six attached loaves in clean newspaper (wrapping paper was not plentiful in 1906) and tied it up with string from packages that had come from the stores. Then two of my older brothers, aged eight and ten, and I felt quite proud when we were allowed to carry the packages down to the depot to be loaded into the boxcar.

(I see I have forgotten to mention that the town's small two-room schoolhouse—with two teachers for the 75 or 80 pupils in the eight grades—was also damaged that April Wednesday morning by the earthquake, and carpenters and glaziers were called in to make repairs. So classes did not resume until the following Monday, and this extra school holiday only added zest to the excitement of us youngsters who were watching the relief food go into the boxcars.)

By this time the food emergency in San Francisco was pretty well known to all the people of the Russian River Valley—as well as to most of the rest of the civilized world. Some of the San Francisco newspapers, which had many subscribers in Sonoma County, were now being printed in Oakland and were coming through by way of Vallejo and Sonoma; and the Santa Rosa dailies were also bringing in reports of the extent of the holocaust.

So it was that the farmers and their wives, even from the most distant farms in that section of the valley, brought in their contributions—more sacks of potatoes and dried fruits, plus hundreds of quarts of "canned" fruits and vegetables. Dressed and roasted chickens were hauled in by the dozens. Pigs, calves, and lambs were slaughtered and dressed—and added to the store in the boxcar. Ed Cook, my father's close friend who ran Geyserville's butcher shop (we didn't call it a meat market in those days), donated a quarter of beef or a dressed hog each day.

This went on for many days, with a new boxcar arriving empty in the morning and going south filled again at night. Just how long this continued I do not recall exactly, but I believe it was more than a week, probably 10 or 12 days—until word came that large shipments, even whole trainloads, of donated relief food and supplies from other states clear to the east coast were beginning to arrive in San Francisco. Please remember that I was only six years old when all of this happened—and it never occurred to me to jot down any of it until over 60 years later. In fact, I feel that time has, if anything, only blurred my memory of what a remarkable and wonderful phenomenon my childish eyes were permitted to witness!

None of the people of our small community were rich. Some of them owned their farms or homes, but most of them lived "lives of quiet desperation," and never knowing what it was like to be without worry over bills and debts, rent and mortgages. (Our family was one of the latter.) All these people had to work, and work hard and constantly, to earn a living—and expected to do so to the end of their days. Yet practically every family unhesitatingly shared what it had with the disaster victims of San Francisco.

From 1906 to the present time I have never heard this story told, nor come across anything about it in print. It is most likely that other railroads and also shipping lines carried out programs of gathering and transporting food and supplies for the hungry and homeless in San Francisco. Likewise, I doubt very much if any community in California, or in neighboring states too for that matter, failed to send help in some form—money, food, clothing, bedding, etc.

But I saw with my own eyes what happened in one small farming community, and I knew that something similarly wonderful was happening in many neighboring communities. And I now realize that when I was very, very young—too young to be aware of it at the time—I was fortunate enough to have had a good look at man at his best.

Pithole

by Robert G. Anderson

Along the banks of Pithole Creek in Western Pennsylvania lies a deserted field overgrown with weeds. In the mid-1800s it was the same. A casual glance might suggest that the place had not changed in the intervening years, but closer inspection reveals forgotten remnants of the once thriving city of Pithole. Pithole's life span was but a few years. Yet, in its heyday, the city was as well-known as Pittsburgh, Detroit, or any other industrial center.

It all began in 1859 when Edwin L. Drake drilled the first successful oil well near the small town of Titusville in Western Pennsylvania. That was the beginning of a new industry—petroleum. The success of "Colonel" Drake at Titusville led to further oil drilling along Oil Creek, and during the Civil War that area grew rapidly.

Then, in 1864 a venturesome driller, I. G. Frazier, leased a farm seven miles up Pithole Creek, quite distant from the Oil Creek producing area. Early the following January, at a depth of 600 feet, he brought in a well producing 650 barrels of oil a day. The report of the new discovery brought wild speculation, but the winter was too severe for immediate new drilling.

The town was created the following spring. Thousands of people—drillers, speculators, teamsters, merchants, and Civil War veterans—came to Pithole to seek their fortunes.

The town literally "sprang up." Two days after lots in the town were offered for lease, the first building was under construction. Six days later, the Oil City *Register* reported that "nearly two entire streets are built up, and a large number of buildings are in the course of construction." Pithole's first hotel, the Astor House, was built in a single day.

This feverish pace continued through the summer. Streets were laid out, a water works system installed, a fire department organized; and there were two each of banks, telegraph offices, and churches. A

Mr. Anderson, a long-time member of the senior staff of The Foundation for Economic Education, retired in 1992. This article is reprinted from *The Freeman,* March 1962.

daily newspaper was published. There were over fifty hotels, one of which—the four-story Chase Hotel—was built at a cost of $100,000.

No census was ever taken of Pithole's population. But by July of 1865 its post office was handling 5,000 letters daily, a volume exceeded in Pennsylvania at that time in only Philadelphia and Pittsburgh. One-third of the production of petroleum in the United States that year came from Pithole. Today, by comparison, it takes practically all of Texas to produce a third of the nation's annual output.

Pithole's Decline

Pithole was an important city in 1865. Scores of new businesses had been created. Some actually produced oil, while the others thrived off the wealth that the wells created. Then the inevitable happened. In 1866, Pithole wells started going dry, and fewer new wells were coming in. At the same time, new fields were being discovered in such places as Pleasantville, Tidioute, and Shamburg. A mass exodus took place. The drillers and speculators were followed by the teamsters and merchants. Buildings were torn down to be moved and rebuilt in other towns. Some were sold for kindling. Fires claimed much of the town.

By June of 1868, oil production had come to a standstill, with only a handful of "hangers-on" in the dying town. Today, Pithole is gone, and many people living in the locality have never heard of it.

In 1866 Pithole became, in modern terminology, a depressed area. Not only were the wells drying up, but crude oil that had been selling in 1864 for $12.00 a barrel declined to a low of $1.35 in 1866. Such low prices forced many oil-producing companies out of business. Thousands of laborers were unemployed. Pithole undoubtedly was the most depressed area of that period of general depression.

Much is heard nowadays about depressed areas in the United States. Newspapers picture shabby homes and families and tell of jobless workers and their hungry children. But they go on to report federal aid to the rescue, and herald the President's "coupon plan" as having struck at the "real root" of the problem.

There was no large government to come forth with aid and assistance at Pithole's time of need. But suppose there had been; consider what might have happened!

One possibility would have been government purchase of crude oil—price support via an "oil bank"—with barrels of surplus crude oil as wheat is stored today. Or, the government could have subsidized the Oil City and Pithole Railroad—just in case it might be needed for national defense. Had there been sufficient unemployment compensation and gifts of food, Pithole might still be populated today.

No one knows for sure what might have happened to Pithole and the petroleum business if government had intervened, but we do know what happened otherwise. A city disappeared because it no longer had economic value or reason to exist. And an infant petroleum industry expanded its annual output from 2.5 million barrels in 1865 to 2.5 billion barrels in 1959. If government had intervened to "protect" them, it might have saved the dying Pithole; but who knows what "help" of this kind could have done to the emerging oil industry?

There are at least three ways in which a so-called depressed area develops: (1) the goods or services it offers may be available elsewhere at less cost; (2) the goods or services it offers may no longer be wanted; (3) the area may have lost its capacity to produce. Pithole qualified in all three ways: its oil wells were drying up, oil was being produced more economically elsewhere, and—without its oil wells—there was no longer any use for the hotels and other services in the town.

It would have been possible, no doubt, to pump tax-collected funds into Pithole, to drill more wells or deeper ones, to subsidize various service industries, and otherwise nurse and coddle that dying community. But would it have been worthwhile to thus defy the market demand for change and progress?

A depressed area is a sign of inefficiency and of failure to satisfy the most urgent and always changing demands of consumers. It is a sign that capital and managerial talent have turned to new and better opportunities to satisfy consumers and earn profits. And it is both an invitation and a challenge to workmen to follow suit.

When government tries to defy such change, it penalizes efficiency and rewards failure, pours good money after bad, and changes the name and character of the subsidized community from Pithole to "rathole"!

The Rise and Fall of the Edsel

by Anthony Young

Mention "Edsel" to anyone over the age of thirty and you will hear pretty much the same response. While the answers may vary somewhat, practically everyone knows it was a car introduced in the 1950s that failed miserably. Many people will add that they think it bombed because of its bizarre front-end styling. But, in fact, the Edsel failed for more fundamental reasons.

The Edsel proved that mere size doesn't insulate corporate decision-makers from errors in judgment; large automotive corporations are just as capable of making major mistakes in new product planning, production, advertising, and marketing as smaller companies. It is a fascinating story that holds free-market implications worth remembering.

The early 1950s were a euphoric period for automakers. In 1955 Americans bought a record 7,169,908 new cars. This auto-buying frenzy was just one aspect of the postwar economy that Vance Packard described in *The Status Seekers,* published in 1959.[1] In Packard's view, automobiles evolved from mere transportation vehicles just after World War II to symbols of middle-class affluence in the first half of the 1950s. The V-8 engine reigned supreme and horsepower was the watchword. In this heady market atmosphere Ford Motor Company conceived a new car that they hoped would help the company surpass General Motors in overall market share.

Seeds of Disaster

Ford executives attributed General Motors' large market share to GM's wide range of offerings—from the low-priced Chevrolet and Pontiac, to the mid-priced Buick and Oldsmobile, up to the luxury-priced Cadillac. Henry Ford II and Board Chairman Ernest Breech believed that the low-priced Ford, upper-middle-priced Mercury, and

---

Mr. Young, a regular contributor to *Automobile Quarterly,* has written extensively on automotive history. This article is reprinted from *The Freeman,* September 1989.

luxury-priced Lincoln car lines left a gap Ford should fill. A 1952 market study confirming this made the rounds at Ford and Lincoln-Mercury division headquarters. The new car should be for the young executive. By 1954, a task force drew up plans for a medium-priced car to be sold through Lincoln-Mercury dealers.

One top-level Ford executive, Lewis D. Crusoe, disagreed with the proposal, stating strongly that the new car should be a product of a whole new Ford division with its own dealer network. Henry Ford II and Ernest Breech agreed with Crusoe. This was the first key mistake in the Edsel saga and perhaps the most damaging.

The Ford Motor Company was restructured so that there would be distinct divisions for Ford, Mercury, Lincoln, and the yet-to-be-named mid-priced car division. In the summer of 1955, the staff for the new "E" (experimental) car division was brought together in some inconspicuous buildings that had made up the short-lived Continental Division.

What's in a Name?

One of the first jobs for division president Dick Krafve was to select a name for the division and the models to be built. The task was fraught with peril. As author Robert Lacey put it, "The name had to excite the public while not alarming it unduly. It had to distance the new vehicle from existing Ford, Lincoln, and Mercury labels, while remaining reassuringly part of the same great family of automobiles. It had to satisfy all manner of other requirements, from starting with a letter that would look good on the front hood ornament, to not rhyming with anything rude."[2]

Market research had played a key role in developing both the concept and the name of the highly successful Ford Thunderbird, introduced in the fall of 1954. Ford again drew upon market research for the names of its new division and models.

Polling was conducted in New York, Chicago, and two small towns in Michigan, asking people not just for ideas, but what came to mind when certain names were suggested. The possibilities numbered 2,000. Foote, Cone and Belding, the new division's ad agency, ran a contest with its employees that produced 8,000 suggestions, later pared down to 6,000 names. In an effort to get new direction, the head of Ford market research contacted poet Marianne Moore, asking her to come up with names that would evoke "some visceral feeling of elegance, fleetness, advanced features and design." Among her more memorable suggestions were Resilient Bullet, Utopian Turtletop, Pastelogram, Mongoose Civique, Andante con Moto, and the Varsity Stroke.[3] Understandably, none of these was adopted.

In a meeting of the Ford Executive Committee in November 1956, exasperation reached its peak. Chairman Ernest Breech finally made the momentous decision. "Why don't we just call it Edsel?" he asked. Edsel Ford was Henry Ford I's only son. Edsel's three sons were William Clay, Benson, and Henry II. All three were opposed to Breech's suggestion, but the name was adopted.

Twelve months of work to come up with just the right name for the division had gone down the tubes. It was a name having significance only to the Ford family, not the man in the street. In fact, during name-association polling, "Edsel" brought forth responses like "Pretzel" and "Weasel." In a terse memo, public relations director for the new division, C. Gayle Warnock, typed, "We have just lost 200,000 sales."[4]

The names for the various Edsel models were chosen from a final master list having positive connotations. They were Pacer, Citation, Corsair, Ranger, and for the three station wagons, Roundup, Villager, and Bermuda.

The Recognition Factor

The styling of the Edsel is surely the most remembered aspect of the car. This, too, had a depressing effect on sales. Why did it end up looking the way it did?

The original Edsel took shape in the Ford Design Center and was kept under tight wraps. To begin with, photographs were taken of the front-end of every new domestic car. Although differing to a greater or lesser degree, all had basically the same horizontal design theme. The design chief for the Edsel proposed a vertical theme to give it the recognition factor Ford felt an entirely new car needed to set it apart. Lacey wrote, "With concealed airscoops below the bumpers, this first version of the 'E' car was original and dramatic—a dreamlike, ethereal creation which struck those who saw it as the very embodiment of the future."[5]

It was never to be. When all the concessions were made to accommodate cooling, ventilation, production costs, and a host of opinions, the Edsel that emerged in 1957 is sadly the one we remember today. The front-end was likened to an Oldsmobile sucking a lemon, a horse collar—even a toilet seat. The rest of the car, both inside and out, was really no better or worse than the other offerings in the late fifties. Ford achieved the recognition factor it was shooting for, but it wasn't positive recognition.

To build up interest in the new automobile, public relations director Warnock decided on carefully controlled leaks to the print media. These took place over a two-year period prior to the Edsel's introduction. Both *Time* and *Life* made statements to the effect that the mystery car was the first totally new car in 20 years, and that it had been in the planning stages for 10 years. This was patently false. Far from being revolutionary, the Edsel borrowed heavily from both Ford and Mercury components.

In fact, during the first year of production, Edsels were built in Ford and Mercury plants. The Ranger and Pacer Edsels (including the Roundup, Villager, and Bermuda station wagons) were built on Ford chassis, and the Corsair and Citation Edsels were built on Mercury chassis. The Edsel division paid Ford and Mercury for each Edsel built. Every 61st car down the Ford or Mercury assembly line was an Edsel, so workers had to reach for parts in separate bins. Mistakes were made and quality on these hastily assembled cars suffered.

This became painfully apparent when Warnock planned to launch the Edsel. Automotive journalists were to drive 75 Edsels from Dearborn, Michigan, to their local Edsel dealers. The cars had to perform without mishap, and couldn't reveal any defects. After all, the car had been the subject of nearly two years of hype, and expectations were high. After a comprehensive testing procedure that took two months to complete, 68 cars were handed over to journalists and driven to their respective destinations. The other seven had to be cannibalized for parts. The average repair bill for each car came to roughly $10,000, which was more than twice the price of the top-of-the-line Edsel.

The Market Yawns

Ford officially introduced the Edsel in September 1957. "There has never been a car like the Edsel," the brochure read. Nearly three million curiosity-seekers visited Edsel showrooms in the first week.

COURTESY FORD MOTOR COMPANY

Dealers pumped the car for all it was worth, but many people were underwhelmed. Aside from the radical styling, consumers couldn't understand what all the hype had been about.

Ford's fledgling automobile couldn't have been introduced at a worse time. The fall of 1957 was marked by a recession that had a severe impact on car sales. Compared to the previous year, Desoto sales plunged 54 percent, Mercury dropped 48 percent, Dodge was off 47 percent, Buick 33 percent, Pontiac 28 percent, and so it went. Ford had considered introducing the Edsel in June instead of September, but decided against it. Thus, only a little over 63,000 Edsels were sold in its first year. Some blamed the recession for the Edsel's poor sales, and this was partly true, but another new car, the American Motors Rambler, sold over 100,000 units in 1957 and twice that in 1958. The Rambler was the right car for the market—the Edsel was not.

Ford made yet another error with the Edsel. The company had introduced the snazzy, mid-priced Ford Fairlane in 1956, undercutting the Edsel's market segment. The Fairlane sold for less than the Edsel, and many car buyers who wanted a Ford product saw the car as a better value.

In an effort to cut its losses, Ford merged the Edsel division with Lincoln-Mercury and, for 1959, cut back on available models, added an optional six-cylinder engine, and altered the car's styling somewhat. Plans already were in motion to revamp the Edsel's look for 1960. Just under 45,000 Edsels were sold in 1959.

Even as the completely restyled 1960 Edsels were rolling down the assembly line, the decision had been made to cease production. Only 2,846 units were sold in the car's third and last year.

Market Lessons

The Edsel serves as a textbook example of corporate presumption and disregard for market realities. It also demonstrates that advertising and pre-delivery hype have their limits in inducing consumers to buy a new and unproven car. In a free-market economy, it is the car-buying public, not the manufacturer, that determines the success or failure of an automobile. A manufacturer shouldn't oversell a new car, or unrealistic expectations will be built up in the minds of consumers. If the newly introduced car doesn't live up to expectations, it is practically doomed on the showroom floor.

Ford learned from the Edsel that it couldn't dictate to consumers what they should buy. It hasn't made a similar mistake since. Several years after the Edsel's demise, Ford introduced the Mustang, a brand-new, sporty, affordable car Americans eagerly embraced. More recently, Ford introduced the Taurus, again a response to the car buyer's needs and wants, which has proved a tremendous market success. The Edsel, on the other hand, will remain an automotive oddity—the answer to a question nobody asked.

---

1. Vance Packard, *The Status Seekers* (New York: David McKay Company, 1959), pp. 312–316.
2. Robert Lacey, *Ford: The Men and the Machine* (Boston: Little, Brown and Company, 1986), p. 481.
3. Len Frank, "The Edsel: It Really Was That Bad," *Collectible Automobile,* July 1984, p. 62.
4. Lacey, pp. 483–484.
5. *Ibid.,* p. 481.

III. OBSTACLES TO FREEDOM

The Progressive Income Tax

by John Chamberlain

Expenditures, says Parkinson in his famous Law, always rise to meet income.

It is too bad that Parkinson, that canny man, wasn't around way back in 1913 when the progressive income tax was first adopted in America. If he had been on the scene, he might have shocked at least a few people into sobriety by observing that his Law, as it applies to government, must be phrased this way: "The expenditures of the State always rise to meet *potential income*." In other words, the politico, with the people's total earnings at his potential legal disposal, will inevitably move toward taking it all. In return for votes the politico will, of course, hand most of it back as welfare—or as legalized patronage. But even in handing it back there will be strings attached to it: following Galbraith, the politico will tell the people how the money is to be spent.

Looking back on 1913, one can only be amazed at the incredible innocence of that generation of Americans. When the Sixteenth (the progressive income tax) Amendment to the Constitution was formally ratified, the Congress responded by adding a seemingly quite inoffensive federal income-tax rider to the Underwood Tariff Act. The rider called for rates running up to a maximum of seven percent on the last bracket of a $500,000-a-year income.

Although the principle of the income tax had been subject to a long controversy (it had been declared unconstitutional by the Supreme Court in 1894), the legislators took it lightly. When famed attorney Joseph Choate remarked ominously that, in time, the tax could go to 50 percent or even higher, Senator William E. Borah arose and shook his massive head. The very idea that anyone could ever be taxed at a 50 percent rate seemed silly to the Progressive Republican from Idaho. Hurling his rhetoric directly at Choate, Borah asked: "Whose equity, sense of fairness, of justice . . . does he question?"

Mr. Chamberlain, an honorary trustee of The Foundation for Economic Education, has reviewed books for *The Freeman* since the 1950s in his regular column, A Reviewer's Notebook. This article appeared in the November 1961 issue of *The Freeman*.

As things have turned out, Joseph Choate was altogether too moderate a prophet: today [1961] the top income tax rate is 91 percent, and the 50 percent rate begins at the $16,000-a-year level. In 1913 dollars, $16,000 a year is worth a mere $5,350. During World War I the tax took its first swift leap upward, only to fall back after the Peace of Versailles. Ever since the revenue act of 1934 first turned the full fury of a depression-ridden generation on anyone and everyone with an income of $25,000 a year or more, the rates at the top have been deadly.

The change in the tax temperature over the span of the past thirty years can be most graphically perceived if we consider what a Babe Ruth would have to be paid today to give him a take-home purchasing power comparable to his 1931 earnings. Out of a salary of $80,000 in 1931, Babe Ruth had $68,535 after federal income taxes. If "The Babe" were alive in 1961, he would need a salary of about $960,000 to give him as much purchasing power, after inflation and other federal income taxes, as he had in 1931.

Early Warnings

Long before Joseph Choate voiced his prophecy, English economists were taking a dim view of what might happen under progressive taxation. Said Ramsay McCulloch in 1845: "The moment you abandon . . . the cardinal principle of exacting from all individuals the same proportion of their income or their property, you are at sea without rudder or compass and there is no amount of injustice or folly you may not commit." And he continued: "The reasons that made the step be taken in the first instance, backed as they are sure to be by agitation and clamor, will impel you forwards. . . . Why not take 50 percent from the man of two thousand pounds a year, and confiscate all the higher class of incomes before you tax the lower?. . . Graduation is not an evil to be paltered with. . . . The savages described by Montesquieu, who to get at the fruit cut down the tree, are about as good financiers as the advocates of this sort of taxes."

It was only three years after McCulloch's warning that Karl Marx and Frederick Engels, in the *Communist Manifesto,* advocated a heavy progressive tax as a means of despoiling the "bourgeoisie" and softening middle-class society up for the dictatorship of the proletariat. Walter Bagehot, editor of the London *Economist* feared that the Marxians

Joseph Choate
(1832–1917)

would prevail: he predicted that the progressive tax, in combination with the principle of universal suffrage, would result not only in the destruction of the rich but in the very dissipation of the productive capital which gives society (the poor included) its margins of comfort.

The predictions of McCulloch and Bagehot have not yet come to pass in their ultimate direness; maybe they failed to reckon with the adaptability of man. Psychologically speaking, there is obviously some point where the progressive tax must recoil upon itself, destroying the base from which it might hope to achieve a maximum of "take." Just where the point is we cannot tell: there is no way of measuring businesses that are unborn, or energies and creative enthusiasms that simply fail to well up. But when a progressive tax dampens the impulse to generate income, then the tax base itself must narrow and diminishing returns set in.

A Theory of Justice

To make a tax acceptable, it must be levied in accordance with a theory of justice that is an article of faith with the majority. When justice, or the appearance of justice, fails, revolt is inevitable: the Puritan Revolution in England, the American Revolution of 1776, and the French Revolution of 1789 are all cases in point. The theory of justice behind the progressive income tax is that it imposes "equality of sacrifice"—and as long as this is believed, the tax will be palatable to a majority. "Equality of sacrifice" is the democratic way.

Time was when the progressive tax would not have been accepted as equitable even by a majority of the poor. Traditional equity required that taxes should be levied proportionately, not progressively. This was in accordance with the belief that a man's property, or his income, was an index of deserving achievement, or of value contributed in the marketplace to society. True, some men inherited their property or incomes—but that was something to be handled or regulated under laws of inheritance. In any case the erosion of time could be counted on to take care of the inefficient use of inherited fortune—"shirtsleeves to shirtsleeves in three generations" expressed the common wisdom in this matter of luck in the choice of one's parents.

Under the proportional theory of tax equity, a rich man would pay more taxes than a poor man, naturally. But every dollar of assessed property value, or of income, or of spending, would be taxed in equal amounts at flat percentage rates. Dollars would be treated equally, no matter who owned them, or spent them. Thus the citizens would be accorded the "equal protection of the laws"—and his "privileges and immunities" would be equal, as provided for in the United States Constitution. Any other way of treating taxation was regarded as discriminatory, or as putting penalties on ability, ambition, and success.

It was Marxian socialism—"From each according to his abilities, to each according to his needs"—which fathered the great attack on proportional tax equity: a "heavy graduated income tax" is a salient feature of the *Communist Manifesto* of 1848. But the Marxians would have made little headway if non-Marxian economists had not come unwittingly to their support with the theory that "it is not equal to treat unequals equally." In cases of charity, this is undoubtedly true, but no comprehensive legal system can be reared on a rule which begins by regarding everybody as an exception.

The Value of the Last Dollar

To rationalize their inapposite view, these economists sought the support of "marginal utility" analysis; they argued that the "utility" of the rich man's "last dollar of income" must be considerably less to him than the utility of the poor man's last dollar to the poor man. To take *more* of what the rich man valued less was, to these economists, a way of achieving tax justice. They based their theory of tax gradation from bracket to bracket on the old pleasure-pain calculus of the English utilitarian philosophers: obviously, so they said, there must be more pleasure and pain involved in satisfying (or in failing to satisfy) basic hungers than in buying a Rolls-Royce or subscribing for a seasonal box at the opera. By taking more of the supposedly less-valued "Rolls-Royce dollar" than of the highly valued bread-and-beer dollar, "equality of sacrifice" could theoretically be translated into a law which would satisfy the ethical sense of the majority.

Superficially considered, there is a certain amount of rough practical justice in this way of regarding the "last dollars"—or the upper brackets—of a man's income. If it is merely a question of satisfying the basic hungers for food, shelter, clothing, and the minimal cultural decencies, "last dollars" undoubtedly mean much; they may even mean life and death. But this is an argument for a basic exemption from taxation, not for levying progressively steeper surtaxes in the middle and upper brackets.

Beyond a certain subsistence and cultural minimum, the idea that "last dollars" can be rated in accordance with a scale of "marginal utility" to the individual becomes a fiction. Since men differ by inherited temperament, by circumstance, by ambition, and by training, every living human being values his "last dollars" differently. If intensity of avarice could be measured, the French peasant clutching his franc of profit and Hetty Green clutching her millions might come out at the same place. A Huckleberry Finn—or an ascetic St. Simeon Stylites seated on his column—will care little enough even for a "first dollar," whereas a Major Armstrong, intent on raising the money needed to protect his patent rights to a radio amplifier, may desperately value—and need—his "last million."

Who is to say whether the "last dollar" of a poor man taking a flyer on the "daily double" at the racetrack is worth more to the individual than the "last dollar" of a biochemist who wishes to buy a year's leisure to experiment with rare bacterial cultures? Who is to say whether the last dollar spent by a housewife on a new Easter hat is worth more to its owner than the last dollar thrown into the kitty by a Rockefeller to plant Easter lilies or tulips at Rockefeller Center?

"Equality of Sacrifice"

Money has such protean uses that its personal valuation can take a thousand-and-one turns. It can command leisure, freedom, security, adventure, education, veneration, esthetic gratification, and appendicitis operations—plus the whole economic gamut of ordinary goods and services. It can command both power and the protection of the individual against power. As a cynical wit has put it, though you may be able in some instances to buy happiness with money, you can't buy money with happiness—which could conceivably give the "last dollar" of income a "one-up" position even to a man in love.

To make the attempt to force "equality of sacrifice" by taking *more* of what the well-to-do man presumptively values *less* is, then, to pursue a chimera into a quagmire. The utility of a dollar—*any* dollar—to an individual is a purely subjective phenomenon, and cannot be measured in any known unit. One cannot multiply quantities by qualities and get a mathematically respectable answer, as Sir Isaac Newton observed long ago. To suppose that anybody values his "last dollars" less than anybody else is to substitute mind-reading (and emotion-reading) for objective measurement. It puts a self-righteous and wholly tyrannical power into the hands of a majority, or into the hands of the politicians who represent what they think is the majority.

As for the value of an individual's last dollar to society, this depends wholly on the uses to which it is put. It is the responsibility, the ingenuity, and the creativity of the individual which establishes the social "marginal utility" of the last dollar of income. But here, also, utility cannot be expressed in *a priori* terms, by taxing a man because he might waste his tax dollars.

The pleasure-pain calculus is wholly impotent when it comes to comparing a poor man's ticket to the dog races (theoretically of little use to society) and a rich man's investment in a job-creating business. Or, for that matter, the poor man's contribution to the Red Cross and the rich man's evening dissipation at the Copacabana. Even where the comparisons are freighted with seemingly unarguable moral distinctions, there are quicksands within quicksands. A night club might support a struggling musician while he is composing a great rhapsody, and a dog track could conceivably lead to far-reaching discoveries in canine genetics. On the other hand, charity—or a newly created industry—may result in prodigious waste.

Marginal Utility

Used in price analysis, marginal utility has something objective to work on: the amount of goods which clear the market when the price is either raised or lowered. By utilizing theoretical supply-and-demand curves, one can even make reasonable guesses about the future. But marginal utility, which is of no use whatsoever in judging the intensity of personal feelings, cannot legitimately be used to give society a right to political dictation of the social uses of "last dollars." To tax possible investment capital on the theory that "society," as represented by government, might invest it better is to indulge in a wild guess. Measurement (via a tax) cannot be undertaken *before* the dollars are spent. This is why men have traditionally been left the use of their dollars to spend them or to invest them as they please. When the market decides, there is no uncertainty about the comparative rating of men's desires.

An Equality of Misery

Equality is an idea that leads inevitably to contradictions, depending on the values of the individual who advocates it. One can begin with the theory that everyone should start with the same advantages in life: such advantages as equality before God and the law, equal opportunity for education, and a basic subsistence that will keep one from being warped or stunted during the growing period. This is an idea of equality that is firmly imbedded in the American dream; it has also been roughly attainable in American practice. Granted this equality, however, people who are clever, able, persistent, or merely persuasive must soon outdistance the rest. As a people we have accepted this, traditionally, as being eminently fair.

It does not, however, result in an equalitarian society. Does true equality consist, then, of pulling everyone who has exceptional abilities back into the pack at stated intervals? Does it entail the consistent discouragement of excellence by means of periodic cancellation or retraction of rewards? If it does, then mankind must automatically be deprived of the benefits normally accruing to it from the natural variation of human beings. With the fostering of a widespread "what's the use" attitude, new inventions, new qualitative changes, new theories, ideas, and fashions, must falter; the standard of living must recede; the birth rate must drop; and the equality thus achieved will be an equality of misery.

Insofar as it results in "equality," the progressive income tax is a spawn of the second idea. It attempts to pull the exceptional at least part way back into the pack by canceling a good part of the previous year's gain every April 15. Since it is not a tax on capital, the progressive income tax cannot do the whole job of diffusing a more or less complete equalitarianism throughout society. But it keeps newcomers from amassing capital on their own out of savings—and, taken in conjunction with stiff inheritance taxes, it could carry out a revolutionary job of leveling within the space of a few generations.

How "moral" is this approach to equality via the tax collector? If the end to be achieved were a benevolent brotherhood, then there might be something to be said for it. But the means are neither relevant to nor consistent with such an end. Equality via the tax collector operates through the social motive of envy, not love or charity. It begins with the politics of "soak the rich." Soon the definition of "rich" is expanded to include the middle classes. And it all ends with the exaltation of the bureaucrat, who is in charge of spending the spoils. Minorities are inevitably put at the mercy of majorities—and everybody is at the mercy of the politicos, who get first whack at the resources of the State.

Injecting a Psychology of Depredation into Society

Instead of fostering brotherhood, then, the progressive income tax introduces a psychology of depredation into society. Pressure groups everywhere go for their share of the spoils. The arid states want big dams—at the expense, not of willing investors, but of the common people who have chosen to stay in greener, though more densely populated, New Jersey and Connecticut. Everyone has his pet scheme for spending other people's money, and empires grow in Washington as the politicos cater to the schemers. As money income is taxed away, there is a tremendous competition to get income in terms of social services (untaxed). The State is called upon to provide more money for schools, medical services, pensions, what-not. Producers, who have their own corporate income taxes to worry about, struggle for special tax write-offs; every different productive group, from agriculture to labor, wants exemptions. The result is an intense materialism which is rendered all the more ugly because it puts guns into the hands of any group which thinks it has a chance of transforming a minority into a majority by the mere offer of a trade in votes.

The depredation psychology has its reflex within voluntary associations which are compelled to sly expedients in order to retain assets, earning capacity, or mere utility. Businesses are diverted from thinking about productivity; decisions are often made with a primary eye to "tax advantage."

Take the case of a small sponge rubber company in Connecticut's Naugatuck Valley, for example. It has been built up by hard-working partners. But the partners find their only way of cashing in on their creation in their old age is via capital gains. So they sell their business to a big Akron, Ohio rubber company, with their sons receiving stock as their inheritance instead of a going share in a family business. A somewhat similar instance of a small business firm disappearing into the maw of a larger, forms the substance of Cameron Hawley's novel *Cash McCall*.

Many a small businessman is tempted to sell out for capital gains rather than continue to work for an annual income. The result is that big companies grow as small family businesses disappear. In the big companies salaries are paid partly in cash, partly in "future income" via such things as pension rights, commitments to retainers for "advisory aid" in the years after retirement, and stock options leading to capital gains. Expense allowances go up as entertainment, housing, car use, medical examinations, and vacations-cum-business trips are all allocated to "business costs." For its own part, labor devotes a great deal of its organizational energy into fighting for "fringe benefits" that will not appear on the ordinary tax forms as income. "Fringe benefits" result in an uneven diffusion of gains among the workers, for, while everybody forgoes a possible raise in order that the company may finance a fringe benefit, not everybody collects on the benefit to the extent of his due.

Undistributed Profits

As a defensive reflex against the depredation psychology, high individual tax rates result in the retention of earnings by corporations. The proof of this is objective: undistributed profits made up some 30 percent of corporate profits after tax in 1929 and some 50 percent in 1959. By leaving potential dividend money in a business, the investor gets a capital appreciation that is taxed at the 25 percent of income limit if he chooses to sell his stock. In addition to helping the shareholder stay out of a higher tax bracket, this also provides a method whereby ownership can duck the effects of double taxation of dividend money. While it may be immaterial to a given company that it chooses to finance its future growth out of retained earnings (or undistributed profits) instead of going into the market for share capital, this method of financing robs the investor of his flexibility of decision. The investor sticks, perforce, to his "old company" instead of surveying the field for new options. And the "old company" may do the diversifying which the investor used to do for himself; it may branch out into unrelated lines, which can have good or bad effects depending on the ability of management to handle diversification within a single corporate set-up. In any event, business must pay some cost for being tax-oriented, not production-oriented. Some efficiency is lost if only because tax lawyers come high.

If the need to defend against a depredation psychology has its subtle effects on voluntary associations, it also puts a premium on slyness as practiced by the individual taxpayer. A well-known book company advertises a "Federal Tax Course" and offers a special report guaranteed to show what deductions can legally be claimed for business expenses on transportation, entertainment, lodging, gifts, theatre tickets, club dues, and bills, and "your wife's expenses if she travels with you." Another special report is advertised as showing how "men in the $20,000 to $100,000 class can virtually cut their tax in two" by dividing income among the family. Income can be transferred to minor children; property used in a business can be turned over to a member of the family and leased back (at a rent deduction); income-producing property can be sold from one member of a family to another to gain a depreciation advantage; and so on. All of this comes under the heading of "tax avoidance," which is perfectly legal. Nevertheless, a great deal of energy is necessarily diverted into the business of defending oneself against the government—a loss of energy which might be put to far more productive purposes, with society the richer for it all around.

Tax-Exempt Securities

Finally, to protect against depredation psychology, the rich seek refuge in tax-exempt bonds. Thus potential risk capital disappears into the sink of dead-horse debt. This is the ultimate commentary on progressively taxing "last dollars." Ironically, it would take a "degressive tax," i.e., one that taxed "last dollars" least, in order to bring money from tax-exempts back into the pool of risk money that should be available to the man with a new idea.

The late Professor Henry Simons of the University of Chicago economics faculty argued that the case for drastic progressions in income taxation "must be rested on the case against inequality." If the human race has a natural interest in human variation, then the case for progressive taxation is indeed "uneasy" (to use the phrase of Walter Blum and Harry Kalven, Jr.). But if equality (in the leveling sense) can by any stretch of the imagination be considered the touchstone of the good society, then the progressive tax falls into place as a relevant means to the achievement of social justice. But it is only *one* relevant means, and if it is left to operate alone it will not achieve its leveling end.

The Sorry Record

For better or worse, the progressive income tax in America has obviously not achieved an equalitarian result. This does not mean, however, that it should be written off as socially innocuous. Instead of introducing a leveling principle into society, it has resulted in some strange distortions of the social pyramid. While it has not produced equality, it has resulted in a very practical denial of the old American ideal of "equality of opportunity."

The reason for this is that it tends to stratify classes as they are. Since it is a tax on income, not a capital levy, it leaves old ownership intact without encouraging new—or additional ownership. The rich (within inheritance tax limits) tend to keep their fortunes. But Joe Doakes can hardly aspire to amassing a fortune—or even a sizeable nest egg—on his own if he attempts to do it out of saving for investment purposes. (The fact that millions have risen into "middle-income status" since the time of the income tax amendment has been due to the fecundity of American production, with its fantastically efficient machine development, not to any "redistribution" effected by the tax.)

What the progressive income tax cannot do is to cut down the money-mobility of the rich. A man with a fortune can protect his equity by moving money about on the board of opportunity. He can invest his money in supermarkets in Venezuela, or buy oil rights in Western Canada, or become a partner in swiftly growing industries such as plastics, electronics, or aviation. Thus he can circumvent the ravages of inflation and expand his fortune via capital gains.

But while the well-to-do have a continuing access to opportunity (which they can also open to their sons by making them partners in expansive situations), the middle classes are denied the chance of building fortunes in the first instance to protect. Under progressive taxation an Averell Harriman, a Joseph P. Kennedy, a John Hay Whitney can keep their financial status (and even become ambassadors to the Court of St. James). But the deck is stacked against the emergence in our times of new ambassadorial material. During the past generation the "middle condition of man" has been ground between the upper and nether millstones of inflation and steeply rising progressive tax rates. Reckoned in terms of "disposable income" in "1939 dollars," the purchasing power of the $18,000-a-year man in 1961 is no more than that of the $6,000-a-year man of 1935. If the middle-income man has been committed to insurance payments, his equity in saving has been cut in half. But the rich, who have invested in the insurance companies, have preserved their equities intact.

Soak the Middle Class

The fairness of the tax even within its own "ability to pay" rationalization is entirely questionable. The tax exempts the poor—or taxes them at such a low rate of progression that it is negligible. And, as we have seen, it tends to exempt the rich, who have ways of compensating for loss of dividends by the capital appreciation route. It is the people in the middle-income brackets who do most of the paying. Thus what started as "soak the rich" has become "soak the middle class."

Moreover, the tax bears down with peculiar cruelty on the erratic earner, who may be compensated in a single high-tax spurt for years of patient effort. An author or a playwright may struggle for a decade to master a technique (or a subject) and then produce a single best-seller. But the gains for which the years have been preparing will not be commensurate with the effort and dedication involved. A doctor spends his young manhood in medical school, internship, and building a practice: then, relatively late in life, his income may hit the stratosphere without leaving him much after taxes for his old age. To gain crude equity for himself, the doctor will, in turn, grade his fees on an "ability to pay" basis, taking more from the rich and less from the poor.

Then there is the case of the public performer whose income is clearly related to the state of his muscular reflexes, or the youthfulness of his (or her) face and figure. Ballplayers are lucky to last in the big leagues (and the big money) after the age of 33 or 34. A Joe Louis may earn millions in a brief heyday as heavyweight champion and then spend his middle age in irretrievable hock to the government for back taxes for the mere sin of having depended on altogether-too-sanguine income tax accountants. A Sugar Ray Robinson may be forced back into the prize ring after retirement to recoup a fortune which will prove to be just another mirage when the tax collector is satisfied. In the case of the professional tennis player, a few years in the big money are the most to which the average good-amateur-turned-pro can aspire.

As for movie stars and Broadway performers, they may be able to make the jump from ingenue charm or youthful agility to middle-age character parts. But not every starlet becomes a continuing star—and in such an event the high earnings of youth will never afford the basis for a middle-age income.

Since the onerousness of the present progressive tax rates are becoming obvious to too many voters, a trade has been proposed: let the many present legal "loopholes" (big expense accounts, the oil depletion allowance, and so on) be closed in return for an across-the-board cut in the progressive rates. Vain delusion! The closing of the "loopholes" will mean more income for government. But (to invoke Parkinson once more), expenditures rise to meet income. So why should the State give any of that "loophole" money back in the form of a tax cut?

The "loophole" money will support lots of bureaucratic jobholders—and as Parkinson's Other Law says, work expands to fill up the time of those available to do it.

No, we as a people are on the rack for having accepted an unjust Constitutional Amendment in the first place. We will remain right where we are until a limitation is placed on the principle of the progressive income tax itself.

Editor's Note: Since Mr. Chamberlain wrote this essay in 1961 the income tax rates have changed. The top marginal tax rate was cut from 91 to 70 percent in 1963 under President Kennedy. Then, in the 1980s, the top marginal rate was slashed from 70 to 28 percent under President Reagan. As Mr. Chamberlain predicted, when taxes on the rich were cut, capital shifted from tax-free bonds and collectibles to industrial and corporate investments. The misery index (inflation plus unemployment) was lower under Presidents Reagan and Kennedy than for any of the post-World War II presidents.

In 1990, President Bush backed, and Congress passed, a proposal to raise the top marginal tax rate from 28 to 31 percent. Immediately, revenue from the top wealth earners, which had steadily risen during the 1980s, declined. The wealthiest one percent of taxpayers paid $115 billion—or 25.5 percent of all personal income taxes—in 1990, and only $109.8 billion—or 24.6 percent of all personal income taxes in 1991. The total revenues from the other 99 percent of taxpayers increased from $297.6 billion to $306 billion from 1990 to 1991. As Mr. Chamberlain observed, "what started as 'soak the rich' has become 'soak the middle class.'" Yet in 1993, President Clinton and Congress hiked the top rate again from 31 percent to 39.6 percent.

Antitrust History: The American Tobacco Case of 1911

by D. T. Armentano

A long accepted assumption in the area of government and business relations is that the "classic" monopoly cases of antitrust history clearly demonstrate the need for, and justify the existence of, the antitrust laws. The impression created by almost all the textbooks on this subject is that the business monopolies or "trusts" indicted in the past were—as the textbook theory suggests—actually raising prices, lowering outputs, exploiting suppliers, driving competitors from the market through predatory practices, and, generally, lowering consumer welfare. Ironically, few if any of these same texts provide the student of antitrust with the necessary empirical information that might allow an independent judgment as to the relative conduct and performance of these "monopolies." For the most part, the student is asked to accept the judgment of the author, without being permitted to scrutinize the "brief for the defendant." Such one-sidedness is the kind of poor economic history that leads, inevitably, to poor public policy.

The following is a brief history of the American tobacco industry, and particularly of the American Tobacco Company, prior to the famous antitrust decision of 1911.[1] Unlike many previous accounts, this one will attempt to explain and evaluate the conduct and performance of the American Tobacco Company in the full context of the tobacco industry between 1890 and 1907. While this history might be interesting for its own sake, the ultimate purpose is to demonstrate that the court decisions against the American Tobacco Company prior to 1911 did *not* turn on any sophisticated economic analysis of that firm's market conduct or performance. The firm was eventually found guilty of violating the Sherman Act, but the decision was *not* a consequence of any serious evaluation of the economic costs and benefits of the firm's activities in the marketplace.

Dr. Armentano is Professor of Economics at the University of Hartford in Connecticut. This article, a chapter from his book *The Myth of Antitrust,* originally appeared in the March 1971 issue of *The Freeman*. It is reprinted here with permission.

James B. Duke
(1856–1925)

Cigarettes in America

Although cigarettes appeared in America in the early 1850s, and were unpopular enough with the government to rate their own special penalty tax of up to $5 per thousand by 1868, there was hardly what could be termed a cigarette-manufacturing industry before the 1880 period.[2] Up to that point, the cigarette business had been concentrated in the New York City area where many small firms employed cheap immigrant labor to "hand-roll" mostly Turkish blends of tobacco. But the raw material was relatively expensive, and the hand-rolling operation was relatively inefficient and costly. Besides, there appeared to be great popular reluctance to accept the small cigarettes. Consequently, the outputs and markets were severely limited. Total output of all "manufactured" cigarettes was never more than 500 million in any one year prior to 1880.

But the rather rapid shift in public taste to Virginia blends of tobacco, the slow adoption of machinery for manufacturing cigarettes, and the extensive use of advertising to popularize particular brands or "blends" of tobacco, changed the industry radically beginning in the 1880s.

The use of rapidly improving machines that manufactured cigarettes quickly drove down the costs of manufacture and placed a profit premium on mechanization. Labor costs alone were reduced from 85 cents per thousand without machines to 2 cents per thousand with machines.[3] While an expert "hand-roller" could make approximately 2,000 smokes a day, a properly operating cigarette machine could make 100,000.[4] A few leased cigarette machines—particularly the "Bonsack" machine—could, in a matter of days, generate the entire yearly output of cigarettes. Thus, almost overnight, the optimum size of an efficient cigarette firm increased manyfold, and almost the entire industry emphasis shifted to creating or expanding demand for particular blends of "manufactured" cigarettes. Advertising and marketing expenditures began in earnest in the late 1880s, and it was not at all surprising to find only five large firms doing most of the trade in manufactured cigarettes by 1889. Though there were hundreds of small cigarette producers (mostly hand-rolled varieties) in that period, the firms of Goodwin and Company, William S. Kimball, Kinney Tobacco, Allen and Binter, and the W. Duke & Sons Company came to dominate the young industry and did an estimated 90 percent of total domestic cigarette sales.[5]

The name of James B. Duke is almost synonymous with cigarettes and the rapid rise of the tobacco industry in this country. Though a relative newcomer to the cigarette industry (he entered in 1882), Duke quickly pushed his firm into industry leadership by rapid mechanization of all his operations and, accordingly, huge advertising schemes to increase demand for his increased outputs.[6] He took huge newspaper ads and rented billboard display space to push "Duke of Durham" and "Cameo" brands; he placed redeemable coupons inside his new and improved cigarette boxes to popularize "Cross Cut" and "Duke's Best"; and he enticed jobbers and retailers with special bonus plans and gimmicks if they would handle and stress his products. This unusual marketing approach was extremely successful, and by 1889 Duke's cigarette firm had over 30 percent of industry output and was netting almost $400,000 a year on gross sales of $4.5 million. Duke's firm was the largest and most profitable firm in the manufactured cigarette industry, and appeared to be growing much more quickly than its rivals could or would.

Consolidation in 1890

In January of 1890, the five leading cigarette firms came together to form the American Tobacco Company and installed J. B. Duke as President. Although competition between the leading firms had been severe in the late 1880s, there is little evidence that the combination was the direct consequence of a "destructive trade war" as some accounts relate.[7] Rather, it was an almost inevitable consequence of the economics of the cigarette industry in 1890.

Potentially, the cigarette industry appeared immensely profitable. The price of leaf tobacco, the raw material, was historically very low (about 4 cents per pound); the cost of manufacture—even with less than optimal utilization of equipment—was extremely low; and the existing market prices for cigarettes were already high enough to allow adequate profits. Two things alone remained to cloud the potential profits picture of the industry: maximum utilization of the largest, most efficient machinery to drive the costs per unit down to an absolute minimum; and an elimination or severe reduction in total advertising expenditures as a percent of total output or sales.

Merger provided both of the last-mentioned economies. Consolidation would allow concentration on those blends of tobacco that could be produced most efficiently. Consolidation would also allow great economies of scale to be realized in advertising expenditures. Thus, production and selling expenditures could be lowered per unit of output, and profits could grow accordingly. A combination or "trust" of small cigarette firms was, thus, a natural and predictable economic arrangement since it was clearly more efficient than a decentralized market structure.

Diversification

Between 1890 and 1907, American Tobacco or the "Tobacco Trust" diversified into a number of related industries. Diversification was to be expected since cigarettes, although extremely profitable, represented only 3 to 5 percent of the entire tobacco industry in 1890.[8]

In addition, the public's changing tastes obsoleted particular brand names and even whole products rapidly and, thus, made any specialization extremely dangerous.[9] Furthermore, there was a distinct prejudice against machine-made cigarettes and sales simply did *not* expand as rapidly as anticipated. While American Tobacco had produced slightly more than 3 billion cigarettes in 1893, it produced only 3.4 billion in 1899 and less than 3 billion annually between 1900 and 1905; American's production of cigarettes in 1907 was only 3.9 billion. Even more importantly, American's share of domestic cigarette sales declined from over 90 percent when the firm was formed in 1890 to 74 percent in 1907.[10]

For the most part, American Tobacco's diversification and growth in the tobacco industry was accomplished through the direct purchase of existing firms with cash or stock. It is estimated that American may have bought as many as 250 firms between 1890 and 1907.[11] A very few of these purchases were competitive cigarette manufacturers—*though the bulk of them were not*. Most of these cigarette purchases were made, apparently, to acquire a successful brand-name, since brand-name loyalty was the greatest asset of any tobacco firm.[12] The bulk of American Tobacco's purchases, however, were firms producing non-cigarette tobacco products. For example, diversification into firms that made smoking tobacco, snuff, plug-chewing tobacco, and cheroots was begun as early as 1891. These tobacco products were noncompetitive with cigarettes and with each other, and had their own particular markets and used their own particular kind of leaf tobacco.[13]

In 1898, after many years of competitive low-price rivalry,[14] American purchased the leading plug manufacturers, including, at a later date, the large and important Liggett & Myers Company. They were subsequently organized into the Continental Tobacco Company, partially owned and completely controlled by Duke and American Tobacco interests. Shortly after, in March, 1899, the Union Tobacco Company—manufacturer of the famous Bull Durham smoking tobacco—was purchased. The American Snuff Company was then organized in March 1901, with a paid-in capital of $23 million, and the stock was paid out to the three leading, formerly independent, snuff manufacturers. The American Cigar Company was also formed in 1901, and became the largest firm in that sector of the tobacco market. In addition, American purchased licorice firms, bag firms, box firms, firms that made cigarette machinery, tin foil, and processed scrap tobacco.

By 1902, American Tobacco was manufacturing and selling a complete line of tobacco and tobacco-related products—including over 100 brands of cigarettes—and over 60 percent of the nation's smoking and chewing tobacco, about 80 percent of the nation's snuff, and 14 percent of its cigars. And when the newly organized Consolidated Tobacco Company, Continental Tobacco Company, and the American Tobacco Company all merged in October 1904, to form the *new* American Tobacco Company, the last phase of the diversification and consolidation of tobacco properties was complete. The American Tobacco Company was now a major factor in *all* phases of the tobacco industry domestically and later nationally (although relatively weak in cigars), and its position would be maintained (and even increased in plug chewing tobacco) until dissolution by the courts in 1911.

The 1890–1910 Period: Acquisitions

Though American Tobacco did acquire many firms in all phases of the tobacco business between 1890 and 1911, the total number of its acquisitions must be put in perspective. While over 200 acquisitions appears high—and creates the impression that only a few independent tobacco firms remained—the tobacco industry contained thousands of independent firms in the period under consideration. While American Tobacco did the great bulk of much of the tobacco industry in a few large manufacturing plants, *thousands* of smaller independent firms sold their products at a profit in the open market in competition with the "Trust."

For example, as many as 300 independent cigarette manufacturers may have existed in 1910;[15] similarly, while the Trust produced a great percentage of the nation's output of smoking tobacco in fewer than 25 plants, there were as many as 3,000 plants manufacturing smoking tobacco in 1910.[16] In addition, the Trust accounted for only about seven of the nation's estimated 70 snuff manufacturing plants.[17] And finally, the American Cigar Company operated just 29 manufacturing operations in 1906, while the cigar industry contained upwards of 20,000 independent firms.[18] Thus, the tobacco industry contained thousands of firms *in spite of* the acquisition activities of the "Trust."

Entry and Economies of Scale

The major reason for the numbers of rival sellers is not difficult to discover. With or without the "Trust," entry into tobacco manufacture was relatively easy. The raw material was available to all at the going market rates and the Trust itself owned *no* tobacco land whatsoever. Anyone who wanted to compete could purchase the available raw materials and attempt to sell his product in the open market. In addition, the Trust possessed neither discriminatory transportation rates or rebates[19] nor any superior production method protected by patent.[20] Thus, it was not surprising to find many independent firms in an industry where neither the raw material nor the efficient means of production were, or could have been, "monopolized."

The major reason for American Tobacco's policy of acquisitions is not difficult to discover either: it made economic sense. For example, much emotional nonsense has been made of the fact that American acquired firms and, subsequently, shut them down.[21] The crucial point, of course, is that American concentrated tobacco production—and particularly cigarette production with only two large plants in New York and Richmond—to achieve quite obvious and substantial scale economies.[22] Most of the acquired facilities were mechanically inefficient, and had been acquired only to secure the immensely more valuable competitive brand name. Once acquired the product itself could be produced more efficiently in American's own modern and efficient facilities. Thus, it made good sense and good economics to close down marginal manufacturing operations, and no tears need be shed for the "dismantled factories." There is no evidence that any of the former owners shed such tears since American Tobacco's terms (stock in the Trust or cash) were admitted to be generous to all concerned. Thus, the plants were not acquired just to shut them down.

Other economies of the acquisition policy were achieved in important though not so obvious ways. For example, American's huge production made the ownership of its own foil, box, and bag firms almost mandatory, and the advantages and savings to be realized by accurate and continuous deliveries of these products made economic sense. Its acquisition of MacAndrews & Forbes and Mell & Rittenhouse, the two leading manufacturers of licorice paste, was predicated on possible economies and on the very real fact that the Japanese-Russian War threatened Near East licorice supplies and, consequently, American Tobacco's expansion of plug tobacco.[23] Independent foil, box, and bag firms still remained in the marketplace, and at least four other manufacturers sold licorice paste independent of the American Tobacco firms. There is also no evidence that American's paste firms refused to sell to anyone who wanted licorice at the going market prices. Thus, this aspect of the vertical integration of American Tobacco was economically logical and certainly cannot be condemned as *necessarily* restraining trade.

American's integration into distribution also realized economies. With the virtual elimination of the middleman, the jobbers' not unhealthy margin could be realized by the tobacco manufacturer.[24] Wholly owned retail establishments could also push particular brands more effectively and become an important advertising and marketing innovation. American Tobacco's United Cigar Stores, the most famous and effective tobacco-product retail chain—with over 1,000 stores by 1910 and at least 300 in New York City alone—were certainly important in this respect.

There were still other more subtle economies. A certain amount of inefficient cross-hauling or cross-freighting was automatically eliminated since American Tobacco could fill orders for finished tobacco products from a number of different manufacturing locations.[25] In those modern factories labored nonunion help, and this saved American from 10 to 20 percent on its wage expenses *vis-à-vis* most of its competitors which employed Tobacco Workers Union labor.[26] The Tobacco Trust could demand prompt settlement of all outstanding accounts (30 days), while it was quite common for smaller manufacturers to wait two to four months for payment.[27] It could employ fewer salesmen per product since many of its brands were long established; orders could even be filled by mail without agents of any sort.[28] Finally, it could employ, and did employ, some of the keenest managers in the industry,[29] and they proceeded to implement and extend the potential economies already discussed above.

Consumers and Competitors

But while the Tobacco Trust enjoyed "economies," what became of the tobacco consumer and of the "Trust's" competitors? Did American Tobacco simply act like a "classical" monopolist by restricting output and raising price? Or did American act like a "predatory" monopolist and use its market power to lower prices, and, consequently, drive its competition from the market? Actually, there is little evidence that American Tobacco followed either monopolistic-like conduct: they neither restricted outputs nor raised prices, nor engaged—as a general rule—in predatory pricing practices designed to eliminate their competition.[30] For example, American Tobacco's cigarettes (per thousand, less tax) sold for $2.77 in 1895, $2.29 in 1902, and $2.20 in 1907; fine cut (per pound, less tax) sold for 27 cents in 1895, 33 cents in 1902, and 30 cents in 1907; smoking tobacco sold for 25 cents (per pound, less tax) in 1895, 26.7 cents in 1902, and 30.1 cents in 1907; plug sold for 15.5 cents (per pound, less tax) in 1895, 27.7 cents in 1902, and 30.4 cents in 1907; and little cigars sold for $4.60 (per thousand, less tax) in 1895, $4.37 in 1902, and $3.60 in 1907.[31] In the same period (1895–1907), the price of leaf tobacco per pound rose from 6 to 10.5 cents.[32] Thus, the pricing record indicated above on tobacco products was accomplished during a period when the price of the essential raw material had increased about 40 percent.

Predatory practices are expensive, and it is not usually profitable to attempt to eliminate competition through this technique. This would be especially true in an industry where entry was relatively easy, where nonprice competitive factors were crucial, and where there were hundreds—even thousands—of competitive sellers already in existence. Such a *general* policy on the part of American Tobacco would have been foolish and foolhardy, and no such *general* policy was attempted. Although there may have been some isolated instances where price-cutting played an important part in merger or consolidation,[33] such practices were not the rule.

The Lower-Court Decision

The comments concerning American Tobacco's efficiency and price policy related above are certainly not original. Amazingly, the same sort of comments can be discovered in a reading of the Circuit Court decision (*U.S.* v. *American Tobacco,* 164 Federal Reporter, 1908) that first determined that American Tobacco had violated the Sherman Act. Although Circuit Judge Lacombe found American guilty of violating the Sherman Act, he stated, with respect to the *economic* issues involved that:

> The record in this case does *not* indicate that there has been any increase in the price of tobacco products to the consumer. There is an *absence* of persuasive evidence that by unfair competition or improper practices independent dealers have been dragooned into giving up their individual enterprises and selling out to the principal defendant.... During the existence of the American Tobacco Company new enterprises have been started, some with small capital, in competition with it, *and have thriven.* The price of leaf tobacco—the raw material—except for one brief period of abnormal conditions, has steadily *increased,* until it has nearly doubled, while at the same time 150,000 additional acres have been devoted to tobacco crops and the consumption of leaf has greatly increased. Through the enterprise of defendant and at a large expense, new markets for American tobacco have been opened or developed in India, China, and elsewhere. (Italics added.)[34]

Circuit Court Judge Noyes, while concurring with Judge Lacombe in American Tobacco's guilt, also appeared to concur in the economic issues involved.

> Insofar as combinations result from the operation of economic principles, it may be doubtful whether they should be stayed at all by legislation.... It may be that the present anti-trust statute should be amended and made applicable only to those combinations which unreasonably restrain trade—that it should draw a line between those combinations which work for good and those which work for evil. But these are all legislative, and not judicial, questions.[35]

It was Judge Ward (dissenting), however, who crystallized the economic issues in the case.

> So far as the volume of trade in tobacco is concerned, the proofs show that it has *enormously increased* from the raw material to the manufactured product since the combinations, and, so far as the price of the product is concerned, that it has *not been increased* to the consumer and has varied *only* as the price of the raw material of leaf tobacco has varied. [Italics added.]
>
> The purpose of the combination was not to restrain trade or present competition ... but, by intelligent economies, to increase the volume and the profits of the business in which the parties engaged....[36]
>
> A perusal of the record satisfied me that their [American Tobacco] purpose and conduct were not illegal or oppressive, but that they strove, as every businessman strives, to increase their business, and that their great success is a natural growth resulting from industry, intelligence, and economy, doubtless largely helped by the volume of business done and the great capital at command.[37]

Yet, although three of the four Circuit Court judges admitted that there *was* evidence to indicate that American Tobacco *was* efficient, had *not* raised prices, *had* expanded outputs, had *not* depressed leaf prices, and had *not* "dragooned" competitors, Judge Coxe joined Judges Lacombe and Noyes in concurring that American Tobacco violated the Sherman Act! Clearly the conduct and economic performance of the defendant had nothing to do with the decision. American Tobacco was convicted *in spite of* its economic record because its mergers and acquisitions inherently restrained trade between the now merged or acquired firms, and *that* violated the Sherman Act as interpreted in 1908. Judge Lacombe made the majority's position explicit:

> [E]very aggregation of individuals or corporations, formerly independent, *immediately upon its formation terminated an existing competition,* whether or not some other competition may subsequently arise. The [Sherman Act] as above construed prohibits *every* contract or combination in restraint of competition. Size is not made the test: two individuals who have been driving rival express wagons between villages in two contiguous states, who enter into a combination to join forces and operate a single line, restrain an existing competition....

> Accepting *this* construction of the statute, as it would seem this Court must accept it, there can be little doubt that it has been violated in this case. . . . The present American Tobacco Company was formed by subsequent merger of the original company with the Continental Tobacco Company and the Consolidated Tobacco Company, and when *that merger* became complete two of its existing competitors in the tobacco business were eliminated.[38] (Italics added.)

It was irrelevant to inquire into the benefits of the combination, argued Judge Lacombe. It was "not material" to consider subsequent business methods or the effect of the combination on production or prices. The fact that American Tobacco had not abused competitors, tobacco growers, or consumers was "immaterial." The only issue that was material was that: "Each one of these purchases of existing concerns complained of in the petition was a contract and combination in restraint of competition existing *when it was entered into* and *that* is sufficient to bring it within the ban of this drastic statute."[39] (Italics added.) And, thus, the three judges (with Judge Ward dissenting) ruled that the American Tobacco Company must be divested.

The Supreme Court Decision of 1911[40]

The Supreme Court decision handed down in the American Tobacco case by Chief Justice Edward White in 1911 is a virtual replay of the Standard Oil decision of the same year. Again, White suggests that a "rule of reason" be applied to the undisputed facts concerning the activities of the American Tobacco Company.[41] But, again, that "rule of reason" does *not* include a careful economic analysis of the Tobacco Trust's conduct-performance in the period under consideration. All the Supreme Court did (again) was to detail the history of the tobacco industry between 1890 and 1907,[42] and infer from these undisputed facts that the intent and "wrongful purpose" of American Tobacco must have been to acquire a monopolistic position in the tobacco industry.[43] This conclusion was "inevitable," said White,[44] and could be "overwhelmingly established" by reference to the following facts: (a) the original combination of cigarette firms in 1890 was "impelled" by a trade war; (b) an "intention existed to use the power of the combination as a vantage ground to further monopolize the trade in tobacco," and the power *was* used, i.e., the "plug and snug wars"; (c) the Trust attempted to conceal the extent of its "control" with secret agreements and bogus independents; (d) American Tobacco's policy of vertical integration served as a "barrier to the entry of others into the tobacco trade"; (e) American Tobacco expended millions of dollars to purchase plants, "not for the purpose of utilizing them, but in order to close them up and render them useless for the purposes of trade"; (f) there were some agreements not to compete between American and some formerly independent tobacco manufacturers.[45] With these "facts" in mind, the conclusion was inevitable: "Indeed, when the results of the undisputed proof which we have stated are fully apprehended, and the wrongful acts which they exhibit are considered, there comes *inevitably to the mind the conviction that it was the danger which it was deemed would arise to individual liberty and the public well-being from acts like those which this record exhibits,* which led the legislative mind to conceive and enact the anti-trust act. . . ." (Italics added.)[46]

But, as has been demonstrated in our review of the American Tobacco Company, whether such "acts" are a danger to "individual liberty" and the "public well-being" *is* a matter of dispute. To *inevitably* infer, for example, that purchasing plants and closing them down endangers liberty or the public well-being, *without an economic analysis of the costs and benefits of such an action,* is an unwarranted and faulty inference. If the agreements to secure these "plants" were voluntarily arrived at, then "individual liberty" was *not* endangered; if the plants closed down by American Tobacco were inefficient, and if the products continued to be produced at larger, more efficient factories, then the danger to the public well-being is *not* obvious. The same kind of questions can be raised about the rest of the "undisputed facts" and "inevitable inferences" in this case.

Conclusion

Unfortunately, the Supreme Court in the American Tobacco case did not choose to analyze the economic issues involved, nor choose to use the rule of reason as an *economic standard* to see whether the public well-being had been harmed. Such an analysis, if performed, would have involved a discussion of prices, outputs, economies associated with merger, growth of competitors (especially in cigarette manufacture), and a host of related issues; no such discussion is discovered in this case. American Tobacco was convicted of violating the Sherman Act because its acts, contracts, agreements, and combinations were of such "an unusual and *wrongful* character as to bring them within the prohibitions of the law."[47] The Circuit Court was directed to devise a plan of dissolving the illegal combination, and "recreating" a new market structure that would not violate the antitrust law.

The fundamental purpose of this study has been to demonstrate that the famous American Tobacco decision of 1911 did not turn on any sort of sophisticated economic analysis of actual market conduct or performance. An even wider purpose, however, has been to suggest by example that structural changes *a priori* prove precious little about consumer welfare and that it is not always safe to assume that "bad" structure leads inevitably to "bad" conduct or "bad" performance. Since the present trend in antitrust thinking appears to be moving toward an almost complete reliance on structural factors,[48] the implicit danger of such an approach should be obvious.

---

1. *United States v. American Tobacco Company,* 221 U.S. 106.

2. For information concerning the cigarette industry prior to 1911, see Meyer Jacobstein, "The Tobacco Industry in the United States," *Columbia University Studies,* Vol. 26 (1907); Richard B. Tennant, *The American Cigarette Industry* (New Haven: Yale University Press, 1950); William H. Nicholls, *Price Policies in the Cigarette Industry* (Nashville: The Vanderbilt University Press, 1951); John W. Jenkins, *James B. Duke: Master Builder* (New York: George H. Doren Company, 1927).

3. Tennant, pp. 17–18.

4. Jenkins, p. 66.

5. Tennant, pp. 19–25.

6. Jenkins, pp. 73–84.

7. Nicholls states flatly that The American Tobacco Company was formed in 1890 following an expensive business war begun by James B. Duke (p. 26). But neither the *Report of U.S. Commissioner of Corporations* (February 1909), which Nicholls indicates was his source, nor the lower court decision against American Tobacco in 1909, appeared to bear this out. See William Z. Ripley, *Trusts, Pools and Corporations,* revised edition (Boston: Ginn & Company, 1916), pp. 269–270; and, see 164 Fed. Reporter 722.

8. Even in the 1900–1904 period, cigarettes, by weight, represented only 2 percent of all tobacco products consumed. See Nicholls, p. 7. Cigarettes did not achieve any sort of national popularity until after World War I.

9. Jenkins, pp. 91–92.

10. *U.S. Research and Brief,* 221 U.S. 106, Appendix "F," p. 318. See also Elliot Jones, *The Trust Problem in the United States* (New York: Macmillan Company, 1923), p. 140. Higher percentage figures in some accounts (83 percent is a common figure for 1907) measure American's share of total output rather than output for domestic consumption.

11. Tennant, p. 27.

12. Jenkins, p. 149.

13. *Transcript of Record,* 221 U. S. 106, Vol. I, p. 254.

14. It was not established at court that American Tobacco started this price war; see 164 Fed. Reporter 723, and 221 U.S. 160.

15. See Nicholls, p. 17. Jones mentions 528 independent plants in 1906.

16. Nicholls, p. 15.

17. *Ibid.*

18. *Ibid.,* p. 13. Also, see Ripley, p. 296.

19. 221 U.S. 129.

20. Jacobstein, p. 101.

21. Clair Wilcox, *Public Policies Towards Business* (Homewood, Ill.: Richard D. Irwin, 1966), says that one of the American's "unfair" methods of competition was buying plants to shut them down (p. 139).

22. *Transcript of Record,* 221 U.S. 106, Vol. I, pp. 208–211.

23. *Ibid.,* pp. 227–231.

24. Tennant, pp. 51–52.

25. Jacobstein, p. 126.

26. *Ibid.,* pp. 125–126.

27. *Ibid.,* p. 127.

28. *Ibid.,* p. 128.

29. *Ibid.,* p. 123.

30. Tennant, pp. 49–57.

31. *U.S. Research and Brief,* 221 U.S. 106, Appendix "P," p. 329.

32. Tennant, p. 53.

33. The "plug war" (1894–1898) is probably the most famous example. During this "war," American sold plug at a loss until the large independent plug manufacturers defaulted. The "independents" came together to form the Continental Tobacco Company whose president was James B. Duke.

But some additional facts complicate an easy interpretation of this "war." In the first place, it was not established that American *started* the "plug war." Secondly, the price reductions were limited to only a few "fighting brands"; while American Tobacco lost money on plug, all the large independent plug manufacturers *continued to earn* a *profit*. Lastly, plug sales increased from 9 million pounds in 1894 to 38 million pounds in 1897. See Tennant, p. 29.

34. *Ibid.,* Fed. Reporter, pp. 702–703.

35. *Ibid.,* p. 712.

36. *Ibid.,* p. 726.

37. *Ibid.,* p. 728.

38. *Ibid.,* p. 702.

39. *Ibid.,* p. 703.

40. *United States* v. *American Tobacco Company* 221 U. S. 105.

41. *Ibid.,* pp. 155, 178–179.

42. *Ibid.,* pp. 155–175.

43. *Ibid.,* pp. 181–184.

44. *Ibid.,* p. 182.

45. *Ibid.,* pp. 182–183.

46. *Ibid.,* p. 183.

47. *Ibid.,* p. 181. (Italics added.)

48. Samuel A. Smith, "Antitrust and the Monopoly Problem: Towards a More Relevant Legal Analysis," *Antitrust Law & Economics Review,* Summer 1969, pp. 19–58.

Edwin Armstrong: Genius of FM Radio

by Jorge Amador

The year 1990 marked the centennial of the birth of Edwin Howard Armstrong. Though his name is recognized by few today, his influence is literally all around us. What makes Armstrong's centennial significant is that, more than any other person, he was responsible for the broadcasting revolution.

Described as one of the last great free-lance "attic inventors," Armstrong is credited not only with originating many of the devices that made it possible to transmit and receive long-distance radio signals, but also with developing one of the major modes of transmission-wide channel frequency modulation, which we know popularly as FM.

Armstrong's story, however, goes beyond that of a great inventor cranking out new gadgets for the good of mankind from the isolation of a lab. For Armstrong's FM radio was nearly killed at birth by a combination of fearful competitors and government. His is a cautionary tale illustrating the power to cripple not just one man's business, but an entire industry, when the state controls access to the basic resources that the industry develops.

His father sold bibles and his mother was a schoolteacher, but from an early age Edwin Armstrong showed great aptitude for mechanical things, and by the time he was 14 he was set on a career in "wireless." Like other amateur radio enthusiasts at the turn of the century, Armstrong put together crude sets from coils and tubes, and spent countless hours in his Yonkers, New York, home listening intently for the faint dots and dashes of faraway Morse Code transmissions.

In 1912, during experiments to increase his set's reception power, Armstrong, then an electrical engineering student at Columbia University, devised an improvement over the existing Audion vacuum tube. The regenerative or "feedback" circuit, his first invention, amplified

---

Jorge Amador is a free-lance writer and editor of *The Pragmatist,* a current-affairs bimonthly. This essay is reprinted from the April 1990 issue of *The Freeman.*

the strength of incoming signals hundreds of times, enough to do away with the bother of earphones and to pick up signals from across the Atlantic.

Six years later, as a captain in the U.S. Army Signal Corps, Armstrong was asked to find a way to intercept German military radio communications, which were transmitted in frequencies too high for Allied receivers. Out of his research came the superheterodyne, another circuit with greatly improved amplification which is still the standard in radio, television, and radar sets. Together, the regenerative and superheterodyne circuits made modern broadcasting possible and secured Armstrong's place in the annals of telecommunications.

Among the select audience to whom Armstrong introduced the regenerative circuit was David Sarnoff, the future president of the Radio Corporation of America. The two became friends. Over the next decade, while Armstrong built his reputation as an inventor, Sarnoff rose to the top of RCA. One day in 1922 Sarnoff, frustrated over the problem of static interference with radio broadcasts, said to Armstrong, "I wish that someone would come up with a little black box to eliminate static."

Armstrong was well aware of the problem. Simple static electricity, such as that caused by lightning and electrical appliances, overwhelmed standard AM signals, and there appeared to be no way to get rid of it. Radio engineers, in fact, were resigned to it, and sought to reduce rather than eliminate static interference. "Static, like the poor, will always be with us," lamented one.

But Armstrong found a way. The scope of this article doesn't permit a technical discussion, but the gist of Armstrong's discovery was this: instead of modulating (varying) the amplitude (strength) of the radio wave, Armstrong proposed to modulate a different aspect, its frequency (hence the term "frequency modulation"). FM transmissions, he discovered, weren't subject to interference from sources of static. The "little black box" was a whole new broadcasting technology.

The Advantages of FM

Armstrong's FM has other important esthetic and economic advantages over AM:

(1) Because it operates on a wider frequency band, FM can repro-

duce almost the entire range of sound audible to the human ear, a feature we call high fidelity.

(2) In a process known as multiplexing, used for instance to provide music for stores and offices, the wider band enables the FM operator to send more than one signal at a time.

(3) Because of the way FM-generated waves propagate through the air, an FM station can serve a greater area than an AM station with the same power, or the same area with less power, making FM stations cheaper to operate.

(4) Yet FM stations on the same frequency can be placed closer together geographically than AM stations, because unlike AM their signals don't interfere with each other. In FM we hear only the stronger station, rarely both at the same time.

In 1933 Armstrong took out four patents on FM and presented Sarnoff and RCA with his invention, hopeful that his friend would take the lead in promoting the revolutionary new medium. RCA decided to test it, and in March 1934 invited Armstrong to set up his equipment at the company's Empire State Building facilities. Performance results exceeded Armstrong's claims.

Then, writes broadcast historian Erik Barnouw, in April 1935 the inventor "was 'politely' asked to remove his equipment. . . . That same month RCA announced its allocation of $1,000,000 for television tests." TV was the new rage; nothing more about FM was forthcoming from RCA for another four years. Armstrong was angry over being induced to waste his time by a company that had no interest in developing his invention.

Determined to show the value of FM, Armstrong asked the Federal Communications Commission (FCC) for spectrum space for further FM experiments and sought permission to build his own station. At hearings in 1936, Sarnoff confirmed Armstrong's suspicions. He testified against allocating space to FM and urged that it be given to television instead.

From RCA's perspective, the matter was simple. As put by Don V. Erickson, author of *Armstrong's Fight for FM Broadcasting,* "RCA did not own the patents on FM. It did own the patents on television." Thus the company stood to keep a greater share of any profits to be made from television than from FM radio. Moreover, since it was a vastly superior radio service, FM represented a threat to established

AM operations—in which RCA, as the parent company of the NBC network, had made great investments.

Thus, explains Erickson, "in almost every overt and covert action, it can be seen that RCA (and the majority of the AM industry) were trying desperately to forestall something that would either cut down, or cut out, their operation." Not least among these efforts was to choke off FM's access to the airwaves, which was controlled by the FCC.

Spectrum Socialism

At this point it is useful to note that this and subsequent fights for spectrum space between FM and television were uniquely a product of government involvement. In the regime of spectrum socialism, under which "the public" is said to "own" the airwaves and a government agency (the FCC) administers them, those who wish to try a new broadcast service, even if they don't propose to take up frequencies currently in use, must go to the FCC for permission to operate.

Absent the FCC, if more than one set of operators wished to use the same general area of the electromagnetic spectrum, they could agree among themselves to divide up the virgin space in question. Or they could simply begin independently to operate at specific frequencies, establish by their use a claim to them as if the frequencies were homesteaded territory, and then if necessary trade or sell frequencies to achieve a consolidated band. In this way, there's room for everybody. Nobody can stake out all the possible frequencies for himself at once, or prevent another from staking out his own space.

Spectrum socialism, however, makes the allocation process controversial. It forces each party to thrash it out at the FCC, where the incentive is to try to get everything that's available. After all, if you must go to the effort and expense of making your case at a hearing—and particularly if you are in competition with others—you might as well ask for all the frequencies at hand, in the hope of ending up with more than you might need. Suddenly there's not enough room for everybody, "justifying" the existence of the allocating agency that encouraged the problem. With this approach, one man's gain becomes another's loss.

The system also gives you the chance to shut out the competition by decree, as RCA attempted. Eventually the FCC allocated television 120 megacycles for experiments, while FM received just 2.7. The agency at first even denied Armstrong a license to build a station, but finally relented in the face of persistent efforts by the inventor.

Armstrong then proceeded to build his station, W2XMN at Alpine, New Jersey, to demonstrate FM's possibilities. Shortly after it began transmitting in July 1939, interest in FM soared. Armstrong commissioned General Electric to build 25 FM receiving sets at his own expense. GE liked the new medium so much that it began to prepare for mass production. The Yankee Network built another station in Massachusetts and began broadcasting in FM to New England.

By the fall of that year, the FCC had more than 150 applications to build FM stations. The space it had parsimoniously allocated to FM three years before was plainly not enough to satisfy existing demand. FM had arrived. Meanwhile, television was a curiosity at the 1939 World's Fair.

As *Fortune* magazine commented in October 1939:

> [W]hile granting the reasonableness of a certain hesitancy, the observer cannot help remarking that the industry has been infuriatingly reactionary in its attitude towards Major Armstrong's development. . . . Moreover, the fact that RCA kept this inventor hanging on the end of a string, without committing itself definitely, was certainly not conducive to progress on the technological frontier. . . .
>
> While the duty of the FCC in making shortwave band allocations was clearly to get television on the air as quickly as possible, the Commission's failure to understand frequency modulation, and to place the proper estimate on its technological importance, is just as deplorable as the industry's failure to push it. . . . What FM needs at the present time above all things is an allocation that will put it on a commercial status and will at the same time be large enough to permit it to operate to full advantage.

On May 20, 1940, the FCC finally gave rein to FM. It took Channel 1 off the television band and allotted it to FM. The Commission assigned FM the frequencies between 42 and 50 megahertz, enough for 40 FM channels, and authorized commercial service beginning January 1, 1941.

The future looked bright for FM. Other radio-set manufacturers, including Zenith and Western Electric (but not RCA, as we shall see), arranged royalty deals. Despite the United States' entry into World War II, the number of commercial FM stations doubled from 18 in 1941 to 36 in 1942, and grew to 46 in 1945. According to *Time* magazine, more than a half-million FM radio receivers were then in use.

Then came a shocker: in January 1945 the FCC proposed to kick FM up into the range of frequencies around 100 megahertz, and to give television additional space in the vacated area. This precipitated a third spectrum battle between FM and television.

The stated reason for the proposed move was the concern that, at FM's current frequencies, radio transmissions would be particularly vulnerable to interference caused by sunspots. It was necessary to make the move immediately, since the height of the next sunspot cycle was expected in 1948–49.

The Commission called hearings for the spring of 1945. It established a Radio Technical Planning Board in several subcommittees to evaluate the proposed general spectrum reallocation. Panel 5, which investigated the claims of sunspot interference, found the evidence lacking and voted 27 to 1 against moving FM. The Board as a whole also recommended against the move.

Armstrong's biographer, Lawrence Lessing, notes that AM interests featured prominently in the pro-FM move camp: "But a long string of witnesses, including representatives of CBS, ABC, Cowles Broadcasting, Crosley, Philco, Motorola, and DuMont, urged that FM be moved 'upstairs.'"

Despite the findings of its own experts and the strenuous opposition of Armstrong and the FM industry, the FCC went ahead with the move in 1945, ostensibly on the basis of the testimony of one engineer who later admitted his calculations had been wrong. The FCC then assigned this band, from which FM radio was banished "for its own good," to television, which Lessing notes was "about twenty-five times more sensitive to any kind of interference than FM and which, moreover, was still required to use FM on its sound channel."

The dreaded interference never showed up, but the effect of the move on FM was disastrous. With one stroke the FCC "made obsolescent every FM radio receiver, every FM transmitter, and a major part of all FM equipment and tubes," writes Erickson. "Thus, with no new FM equipment on the lucrative postwar market and no advertisers to purchase time on the new band of frequencies, FM in its first ten years of existence was brought close to the brink of commercial death." Shortly after the FM shift was proposed, *The New York Times* reported that "The total investment of the country in transmitters, receivers and other [FM] paraphernalia was estimated 'in the region of $50,000,000 to $100,000,000.'" A spokesman for the Frequency Modulation Broadcasters Inc. predicted in February 1945 that the move "would cost prospective buyers of FM receiving sets $100,000,000 more than if they would be permitted to buy sets now designed as soon as they could be made available after the war."

In a brief filed with the FCC, the broadcasters complained that "The change would cost a paralyzing delay during the post-war years when FM could move forward with great rapidity." The delay, in fact, would prove devastating. "FM practically had to start all over again," observed the *Times*' radio critic in 1949. Erickson describes the situation:

> As though [FM was] just invented, equipment had to be put on the drawing board and experimented with to develop sophistication in these very high frequencies; stations had to be reconverted before they could program; and most drastic, the public had to be convinced all over again that FM was worth the purchase of another radio. In this great postwar market, then, AM broadcasting was able to step in and fill part of the great demand for new entertainment, with television coming up a fast second.

"The RCA-NBC forces rejoiced," adds Barnouw. "The new development tended to protect the status quo in radio while providing spectrum space for the expansion of television."

More Controls

The 1945 spectrum shift presaged a series of postwar decisions by the FCC, all founded upon the state's control over the airwaves, which tended further to hamstring the FM industry. That same year the agency approved a "Single Market Plan," proposed by another AM network, the Columbia Broadcasting System, to limit the power and reach of FM stations to a single city or market.

The effect of this was to put FM at a further competitive disadvantage *vis-à-vis* AM. While many AM stations continued to be allowed to send their signals through "clear channels" across the continent, FM stations were prevented from attracting advertiser revenue by serving a wider area.

Radio-set manufacturers were prohibited by the FCC from easing the frequency transition by building sets that could tune in to both the old and the new bands. In April 1951, the Commission prohibited FM stations from multiplexing signals to stores, offices, and other establishments, a nascent source of revenue for cash-starved operators. (The ban was lifted in July 1955.)

Before the war the invisible hand of the market had pointed to a rosy future, but the iron fist of the State nearly choked FM at birth, then pushed it into the broadcasting wilderness for decades. Three years after the spectrum shift, independent FM stations were reporting \$1.1 million in total revenues—and \$4.2 million in expenses, for a staggering loss of three times total revenue. FM's revenue did not approach even half its expenses until 1952, and the industry as a whole did not begin to make a profit until 1976. Television and AM radio enjoyed the fruits of the postwar entertainment market. The number of TV stations jumped from 12 in 1947 to 494 in 1957, and AM stations increased from 1,062 to 3,008. Meanwhile nearly 200 FM stations, which, despite the handicaps, had opened in postwar enthusiasm, found it necessary to close up shop.

RCA, which first ignored FM and then asked the FCC to rule it out of the airwaves, eventually accepted the new medium as a fact of life and started to manufacture FM receivers, as well as televisions with the required FM sound. Sarnoff had offered Armstrong a flat fee of \$1,000,000 for a license to use his FM system when it was first approved for commercial use in 1940, but Armstrong preferred a royalty arrangement. Subsequently RCA tried to negotiate similar deals a number of times, but Armstrong always refused, on the grounds that it would be unfair to other manufacturers who were paying royalties on sales.

However, RCA had a firm policy of making cash settlements.

RCA, writes Barnouw, "did not pay royalties; it collected them." The company patented a rival FM system it claimed was different from Armstrong's, and licensed that to other manufacturers. So, although Edwin Armstrong held the basic patents on frequency modulation, RCA paid him nothing, and instead collected from others. Armstrong's final battle was on.

The inventor published a technical paper showing that RCA's product embodied no new principle and was essentially a copy of his. In July 1948, he sued RCA and NBC for patent infringement.

The pretrial proceedings dragged on for more than five years. "Armstrong, normally patient," writes Barnouw, "became a man possessed. All his energies came to be centered on the suit. Three o'clock in the morning would find him poring over transcripts. At all hours he called attorneys to discuss tactics."

The bitter, protracted struggle diverted Armstrong from his research, spent his fortune and health, and alienated his family and friends, who urged him to settle for his own sake. Late in January 1954, literally sick and tired, Armstrong surrendered. He gave his lawyer the go-ahead to explore a settlement. On the night of January 31, he dressed for the cold night and stepped out—out the window of his 13th-floor New York City apartment. His body was found the next morning. A few months later, RCA paid Armstrong's estate $1,040,000 and the case was closed.

For Further Reading:

Erik Barnouw, *The Golden Web: A History of Broadcasting in the United States 1933–1953* (New York: Oxford University Press, 1968)

Don V. Erickson, *Armstrong's Fight for FM Broadcasting: One Man vs. Big Business and Bureaucracy* (Tuscaloosa: University of Alabama Press, 1973)

Sydney W. Head, *Broadcasting in America: A Survey of Television and Radio* (Boston: Houghton Mifflin, 1972)

Edward A. Herron, *Miracle of the Air Waves: A History of Radio* (New York: Julian Messner, 1969)

Lawrence P. Lessing, *Man of High Fidelity: Edwin Howard Armstrong* (Philadelphia: Lippincott, 1956)

Christopher H. Sterling, *Electronic Media: A Guide to Trends in Broadcasting and Newer Technologies, 1920–1983* (New York: Praeger, 1984)

The Great Depression

by Hans F. Sennholz

Although the Great Depression engulfed the world economy more than 50 years ago, it lives on as a nightmare for individuals old enough to remember and as a frightening specter in the textbooks of our youth. Some 13 million Americans were unemployed, "not wanted" in the production process. One worker out of every four was walking the streets in want and despair. Thousands of banks, hundreds of thousands of businesses, and millions of farmers fell into bankruptcy or ceased operations entirely. Nearly everyone suffered painful losses of wealth and income.

Many Americans are convinced that the Great Depression reflected the breakdown of an old economic order built on unhampered markets, unbridled competition, speculation, property rights, and the profit motive. According to them, the Great Depression proved the inevitability of a new order built on government intervention, political and bureaucratic control, human rights, and government welfare. Such persons, under the influence of Keynes, blame businessmen for precipitating depressions by their selfish refusal to spend enough money to maintain or improve the people's purchasing power. This is why they advocate vast governmental expenditures and deficit spending—resulting in an age of money inflation and credit expansion.

Classical economists learned a different lesson. In their view, the Great Depression consisted of four consecutive depressions rolled into one. The causes of each phase differed, but the consequences were all the same: business stagnation and unemployment.

The Business Cycle

The first phase was a period of boom and bust, like the business cycles that had plagued the American economy in 1819–20, 1839–43,

---

Dr. Sennholz is the President of the Foundation for Economic Education. This article, which originally appeared in the April 1975 issue of *The Freeman,* has been expanded and reprinted as *The Great Depression: Will We Repeat It?* (available from FEE at $4.95 per copy).

1857–60, 1873–78, 1893–97, and 1920–21. In each case, government had generated a boom through easy money and credit, which was soon followed by the inevitable bust.

The spectacular crash of 1929 followed five years of reckless credit expansion by the Federal Reserve System under the Coolidge Administration. In 1924, after a sharp decline in business, the Reserve banks suddenly created some $500 million in new credit, which led to a bank credit expansion of over $4 billion in less than one year. While the immediate effects of this new powerful expansion of the nation's money and credit were seemingly beneficial, initiating a new economic boom and effacing the 1924 decline, the ultimate outcome was most disastrous. It was the beginning of a monetary policy that led to the stock market crash in 1929 and the following depression. In fact, the expansion of Federal Reserve credit in 1924 constituted what Benjamin Anderson in his great treatise on recent economic history (*Economics and the Public Welfare,* D. Van Nostrand, 1949) called "the beginning of the New Deal."

The Federal Reserve credit expansion in 1924 also was designed to assist the Bank of England in its professed desire to maintain prewar exchange rates. The strong U.S. dollar and the weak British pound were to be readjusted to prewar conditions through a policy of inflation in the United States and deflation in Great Britain.

The Federal Reserve System launched a further burst of inflation in 1927, the result being that total currency outside banks plus demand and the deposits in the United States increased from $44.51 billion at the end of June, 1924, to $55.17 billion in 1929. The volume of farm and urban mortgages expanded from $16.8 billion in 1921 to $27.1 billion in 1929. Similar increases occurred in industrial, financial, and state and local government indebtedness. This expansion of money and credit was accompanied by rapidly rising real estate and stock prices. Prices for industrial securities, according to Standard & Poor's common stock index, rose from 59.4 in June of 1922 to 195.2 in September of 1929. Railroad stock climbed from 189.2 to 446.0, while public utilities rose from 82.0 to 375.1.

A Series of False Signals

The vast money and credit expansion by the Coolidge Administration made 1929 inevitable. Inflation and credit expansion always precipitate business maladjustments and malinvestments that must later he liquidated. The expansion artificially reduces and thus falsifies interest rates, and thereby misguides businessmen in their investment decisions. In the belief that declining rates indicate growing supplies of capital savings, they embark upon new production projects. The creation of money gives rise to an economic boom. It causes prices to rise, especially prices of capital goods used for business expansion. But these prices constitute business costs. They soar until business is no longer profitable, at which time the decline begins. In order to prolong the boom, the monetary authorities may continue to inject new money until finally frightened by the prospects of a runaway inflation. The boom that was built on the quicksand of inflation then comes to a sudden end.

The ensuing recession is a period of repair and readjustment. Prices and costs adjust anew to consumer choices and preferences. And above all, interest rates readjust to reflect once more the actual supply of and demand for genuine savings. Poor business investments are abandoned or written down. Business costs, especially labor costs, are reduced through greater labor productivity and managerial efficiency, until business can once more be profitably conducted, capital investments earn interest, and the market economy function smoothly again.

After an abortive attempt at stabilization in the first half of 1928, the Federal Reserve System finally abandoned its easy money policy at the beginning of 1929. It sold government securities and thereby halted the bank credit expansion. It raised its discount rate to 6 percent in August 1929. Time-money rates rose to 8 percent, commercial paper rates to 6 percent, and call rates to the panic figures of 15 percent and 20 percent. The American economy was beginning to readjust. In June 1929, business activity began to recede. Commodity prices began their retreat in July.

The security market reached its high on September 19 and then, under the pressure of early selling, slowly began to decline. For five more weeks the public nevertheless bought heavily on the way down. More than 100 million shares were traded at the New York Stock Exchange in September. Finally it dawned upon more and more stockholders that the trend had changed. Beginning with October 24, 1929, thousands stampeded to sell their holdings immediately and at any price. Avalanches of selling by the public swamped the ticker tape. Prices broke spectacularly.

Liquidation and Adjustment

The stock market break signaled the beginning of a readjustment long overdue. It should have been an orderly liquidation and adjustment followed by a normal revival. After all, the financial structure of business was very strong. Fixed costs were low as business had refunded a good many bond issues and had reduced debts to banks with the proceeds of the sale of stock. In the following months, most business earnings made a reasonable showing. Unemployment in 1930 averaged under 4 million, or 7.8 percent of the labor force.

In modern terminology, the American economy of 1930 had fallen into a mild recession. In the absence of any new causes for depression, the following year should have brought recovery as in previous depressions. In 1921–22 the American economy recovered fully in less than a year. What, then, precipitated the abysmal collapse after 1929? What prevented the price and cost adjustments and thus led to the second phase of the Great Depression?

Disintegration of the World Economy

The Hoover Administration opposed any readjustment. Under the influence of "the new economics" of government planning, the President urged businessmen *not* to cut prices and reduce wages, but rather to increase capital outlay, wages, and other spending in order to maintain purchasing power. He embarked upon deficit spending and called upon municipalities to increase their borrowing for more public works. Through the Farm Board, which Hoover had organized in the autumn of 1929, the federal government tried strenuously to uphold the prices of wheat, cotton, and other farm products. The GOP tradition was further invoked to curtail foreign imports.

The Hawley-Smoot Tariff Act of June 1930, raised American tariffs to unprecedented levels, which practically closed our borders to foreign goods. According to most economic historians, this was the crowning folly of the whole period from 1920 to 1933 and the beginning of the real depression. "Once we raised our tariffs," wrote Benjamin Anderson, "an irresistible movement all over the world to raise tariffs and to erect other trade barriers, including quotas, began. Protectionism ran wild over the world. Markets were cut off. Trade lines were narrowed. Unemployment in the export industries all over the world grew with great rapidity. Farm prices in the United States dropped sharply through the whole of 1930, but the most rapid rate of decline came following the passage of the tariff bill." When President Hoover announced he would sign the bill into law, industrial stocks broke 20 points in one day. The stock market correctly anticipated the depression.

The protectionists have never learned that curtailment of imports inevitably hampers exports. Even if foreign countries do not immediately retaliate for trade restrictions injuring them, their foreign purchases are circumscribed by their ability to sell abroad. This is why the Hawley-Smoot Tariff Act which closed our borders to foreign products also closed foreign markets to our products. American exports fell from $5.5 billion in 1929 to $1.7 billion in 1932. American agriculture customarily had exported over 20 percent of its wheat, 55 percent of its cotton, 40 percent of its tobacco and lard, and many other products. When international trade and commerce were disrupted, American farming collapsed. In fact, the rapidly growing trade restrictions, including tariffs, quotas, foreign exchange controls, and other devices were generating a world-wide depression.

Agricultural commodity prices, which had been well above the 1926 base of 100 before the crisis, dropped to a low of 47 in the summer of 1932. Such prices as $2.50 a hundredweight for hogs, $3.28 for beef cattle, and 32¢ a bushel for wheat plunged hundreds of thousands of farmers into bankruptcy. Farm mortgages were foreclosed until various states passed moratoria laws, thus shifting the bankruptcy to countless creditors.

Rural Banks in Trouble

The main creditors of American farmers were, of course, the rural banks. When agriculture collapsed, the banks closed their doors. Some 2,000 banks with deposit liabilities of over $1.5 billion, suspended operations between August 1931 and February 1932. Those banks that remained open were forced to curtail their operations sharply. They liquidated customers' loans on securities, contracted real estate loans, processed for the payment of old loans, and refused to make new ones. Initially, they dumped their most marketable bond holdings on an already depressed market. The panic that had engulfed American agriculture also gripped the banking system and its millions of customers.

The American banking crisis was aggravated by a series of events involving Europe. When the world economy began to disintegrate and economic nationalism ran rampant, European debtor countries were cast in precarious payment situations. Austria and Germany ceased to make foreign payments and froze large English and American credits; when England finally suspended gold payments in September 1931, the crisis spread to the United States. The fall in foreign bond values set off a collapse of the general bond market, which hit American banks at their weakest point—their investment portfolios.

Nineteen-thirty-one was a tragic year. The whole nation, in fact, the whole world, fell into the cataclysm of despair and depression. American unemployment jumped to more than 8 million and continued to rise. The Hoover Administration, summarily rejecting the thought that it had caused the disaster, labored diligently to place the blame on American businessmen and speculators. President Hoover called together the nation's industrial leaders and pledged them to adopt his program to maintain wage rates and expand construction. He sent a telegram to all the governors, urging cooperative expansion of all public works programs. He expanded federal public works and granted subsidies to suffering farmers, a host of federal agencies embarked upon price stabilization policies that generated ever larger crops and surpluses which in turn depressed product prices even further. Economic conditions went from bad to worse and unemployment in 1932 averaged 12.4 million.

In this dark hour of human want and suffering, the federal government struck a final blow. The Revenue Act of 1932 doubled the income tax, the sharpest increase in the federal tax burden in American history. Exemptions were lowered and "earned income credit" was eliminated. Normal tax rates were raised from a range of 1 1/2 to 5 percent to a range of 4 to 8 percent, surtax rates from 20 percent to a maximum of 55 percent. Corporation tax rates were boosted from 12 percent to 13 3/4 and 14 1/2 percent. Estate taxes were raised. Gift taxes were imposed with rates from 3/4 to 33 1/2 percent. A 1¢ gasoline tax was imposed, a 3 percent automobile tax, a telegraph and telephone tax, a 2¢ check tax, and many other excise taxes. And finally, postal rates were increased substantially.

When state and local governments faced shrinking revenues, they, too, joined the federal government in imposing new levies. The rate schedules of existing taxes on income and business were increased and new taxes imposed on business income property, sales, tobacco, liquor, and other products.

Murray Rothbard, in his authoritative work on *America's Great Depression* (Van Nostrand, 1963), estimates that the fiscal burden of federal, state, and local governments nearly doubled during the period, rising from 16 percent of net private product to 29 percent. This blow, alone, would bring any economy to its knees, and shatters the silly contention that the Great Depression was a consequence of economic freedom.

The New Deal: NRA and AAA

One of the great attributes of the private-property market system is its inherent ability to overcome almost any obstacle. Through price and cost readjustment, managerial efficiency and labor productivity, new savings and investments, the market economy tends to regain its equilibrium and resume its service to consumers. It doubtless would have recovered in short order from the Hoover interventions had there been no further tampering.

However, when President Franklin Delano Roosevelt assumed the Presidency, he, too, fought the economy all the way. In his first 100 days, he swung hard at the profit order. Instead of clearing away the prosperity barriers erected by his predecessor, he built new ones of his own. He struck in every known way at the integrity of the U.S. dollar through quantitative increases and qualitative deterioration. He seized the people's gold holdings and subsequently devalued the dollar by 40 percent.

With some third of industrial workers unemployed, President Roosevelt embarked upon sweeping industrial reorganization. He persuaded Congress to pass the National Industrial Recovery Act (NIRA), which set up the National Recovery Administration (NRA). Its purpose was to get business to regulate itself, ignoring the antitrust laws and developing fair codes of prices, wages, hours, and working conditions. The President's Re-employment Agreement called for a minimum wage of 40¢ an hour ($12 to $15 a week in smaller communities), a 35-hour work week for industrial workers and 40 hours for white-collar workers, and a ban on all youth labor.

This was a naive attempt at "increasing purchasing power" by increasing payrolls. But, the immense increase in business costs through shorter hours and higher wage rates worked naturally as an *antirevival* measure. After passage of the Act, unemployment rose to nearly 13 million. The South, especially, suffered severely from the minimum wage provisions. The Act forced 500,000 Negroes out of work.

Nor did President Roosevelt ignore the disaster that had befallen American agriculture. He attacked the problem by passage of the Farm Relief and Inflation Act, popularly known as the First Agricultural Adjustment Act. The objective was to raise farm income by cutting the acreages planted or destroying the crops in the field, paying the farmers *not* to plant anything, and organizing marketing agreements to improve distribution. The program soon covered not only cotton, but also all principal cash crops. The expenses of the program were to be covered by a new "processing tax" levied on an already depressed industry.

NRA codes and AAA processing taxes came in July and August of 1933. Again, economic production, which had flurried briefly before the deadlines, sharply turned downward. The Federal Reserve business index dropped from 100 in July to 72 in November of 1933.

Pump-Priming Measures

When the economic planners saw their plans go wrong, they simply prescribed additional doses of federal pump priming. In his January 1934 Budget Message, Mr. Roosevelt promised expenditures of $10 billion while revenues were at $3 billion. Yet, the economy failed to revive; the business index rose to 86 in May of 1934, and then turned down again to 71 by September. Furthermore, the spending program caused a panic in the bond market which cast new doubts on American money and banking.

Revenue legislation in 1933 sharply raised income tax rates in the higher brackets and imposed a 5 percent withholding tax on corporate dividends. Tax rates were raised again in 1934. Federal estate taxes were brought to the highest levels in the world. In 1935, federal estate and income taxes were raised once more, although the additional revenue yield was insignificant. The rates seemed clearly aimed at the redistribution of wealth.

According to Benjamin Anderson, "the impact of all these multitudinous measures—industrial, agricultural, financial, monetary and other—upon a bewildered industrial and financial community was extraordinarily heavy. We must add the effect of continuing disquieting utterances by the President. He had castigated the bankers in his inaugural speech. He had made a slurring comparison of British and American bankers in a speech in the summer of 1934. . . . That private enterprise could survive and rally in the midst of so great a disorder is an amazing demonstration of the vitality of private enterprise."

Then came relief from unexpected quarters. The "nine old men" of the Supreme Court, by unanimous decision, outlawed NRA in 1935 and AAA in 1936. The Court maintained that the federal legislative power had been unconstitutionally delegated and states' rights violated.

These two decisions removed some fearful handicaps under which the economy was laboring. NRA, in particular, was a nightmare with continuously changing rules and regulations by a host of government bureaus. Above all, voiding of the act immediately reduced labor costs and raised productivity as it permitted labor markets to adjust. The death of AAA reduced the tax burden of agriculture and halted the shocking destruction of crops. Unemployment began to decline. In 1935 it dropped to 9.5 million, or 18.4 percent of the labor force, and in 1936 to only 7.6 million, or 14.5 percent.

A New Deal for Labor

The third phase of the Great Depression was thus drawing to a close. But there was little time to rejoice, for the scene was being set for another collapse in 1937 and a lingering depression that lasted until the day of Pearl Harbor. More than 10 million Americans were unemployed in 1938, and more than 9 million in 1939.

The relief granted by the Supreme Court was merely temporary. The Washington planners could not leave the economy alone; they had to win the support of organized labor, which was vital for re-election.

The Wagner Act of July 5, 1935, earned the lasting gratitude of labor. This law revolutionized American labor relations. It took labor disputes out of the courts of law and brought them under a newly created federal agency, the National Labor Relations Board, which became prosecutor, judge, and jury, all in one. Labor union sympathizers on the Board further perverted the law that already afforded legal immunities and privileges to labor unions. The United States thereby abandoned a great achievement of Western civilization, equality under the law.

The Wagner Act

The Wagner Act, or National Labor Relations Act, was passed in reaction to the Supreme Court's voiding of NRA and its labor codes. It aimed at crushing all employer resistance to labor unions. Anything an employer might do in self-defense became an "unfair labor practice" punishable by the Board. The law not only obliged employers to deal and bargain with the unions designated as the employees' representatives, later Board decisions also made it unlawful to resist the demands of labor union leaders.

Following the election of 1936, the labor unions began to make ample use of their new powers. Through threats, boycotts, strikes, seizures of plants, and outright violence committed in legal sanctity, they forced millions of workers into membership. Consequently, labor productivity declined and wages were forced upward. Labor strife and disturbance ran wild. Ugly sitdown strikes idled hundreds of plants. In the ensuing months economic activity began to decline and unemployment again rose above the ten million mark.

But the Wagner Act was not the only source of crisis in 1937. President Roosevelt's shocking attempt at packing the Supreme Court, had it been successful, would have subordinated the Judiciary to the Executive. In the U.S. Congress the President's power was unchallenged. Heavy Democratic majorities in both houses, perplexed and frightened by the Great Depression, blindly followed their leader. But when the President strove to assume control over the Judiciary, the American nation rallied against him, and he lost his first political fight in the halls of Congress.

There was also his attempt at controlling the stock market through an ever-increasing number of regulations and investigations by the Securities and Exchange Commission. "Insider" trading was barred, high and inflexible margin requirements imposed and short selling restricted, mainly to prevent repetition of the 1929 stock market crash. Nevertheless the market fell nearly 50 percent from August of 1937 to March of 1938. The American economy again underwent dreadful punishment.

Other Taxes and Controls

Yet other factors contributed to this new and fastest slump in U.S. history. The Undistributed Profits Tax of 1936 struck a heavy blow at profits retained for use in business. Not content with destroying the wealth of the rich through confiscatory income and estate taxation, the administration meant to force the distribution of corporate savings as dividends subject to the high income tax rates. Though the top rate finally imposed on undistributed profits was "only" 27 percent, the new tax succeeded in diverting corporate savings from employment and production to dividend income.

Amidst the new stagnation and unemployment, the President and Congress adopted yet another dangerous piece of New Deal legislation: the Wages and Hours Act or Fair Labor Standards Act of 1938. The law raised minimum wages and reduced the work week in stages to 44, 42, and 40 hours. It provided for time-and-a-half pay for all work over 40 hours per week and regulated other labor conditions. Again, the federal government thus reduced labor productivity and increased labor costs—ample ground for further depression and unemployment.

Throughout this period, the federal government, through its monetary arm, the Federal Reserve System, endeavored to reinflate the economy. Monetary expansion from 1934 to 1941 reached astonishing proportions. The monetary gold of Europe sought refuge from the gathering clouds of political upheaval, boosting American bank reserves to unaccustomed levels. Reserve balances rose from $2.9 billion in January, 1934, to $14.4 billion in January of 1941. And with this growth of member bank reserves, interest rates declined to fantastically low levels. Commercial paper often yielded less than 1 percent, bankers' acceptances from 1/8 percent to 1/4 percent. Treasury bill rates fell to 1/10 of 1 percent and Treasury bonds to some 2 percent. Call loans were pegged at 1 percent and prime customers' loans at 1 1/2 percent. The money market was flooded and interest rates could hardly go lower.

Deep-Rooted Causes

The American economy simply could not recover from these successive onslaughts by first the Republican and then the Democratic administrations. Individual enterprise, the mainspring of unprecedented income and wealth, didn't have a chance.

The calamity of the Great Depression finally gave way to the holocaust of World War II. When more than 10 million able-bodied men had been drafted into the armed services, unemployment ceased to be an economic problem. And when the purchasing power of the dollar had been cut in half through vast budget deficits and currency inflation, American business managed to adjust to the oppressive costs of the Hoover-Roosevelt programs. The radical inflation in fact reduced the real costs of labor and thus generated new employment in the postwar period.

Nothing would be more foolish than to single out the men who led us in those baleful years and condemn them for all the evil that befell us. The ultimate roots of the Great Depression were growing in the hearts and minds of the American people. It is true, they abhorred the painful symptoms of the great dilemma. But the large majority favored and voted for the very policies that made the disaster inevitable: inflation and credit expansion, protective tariffs, labor laws that raised wages and farm laws that raised prices, ever higher taxes on the rich and distribution of their wealth. The seeds for the Great Depression were sown by scholars and teachers during the 1920s and earlier when social and economic ideologies that were hostile toward our traditional order of private property and individual enterprise conquered our colleges and universities. The professors of earlier years were as guilty as the political leaders of the 1930s.

Social and economic decline is facilitated by moral decay. Surely, the Great Depression would be inconceivable without the growth of covetousness and envy of great personal wealth and income, the mounting desire for public assistance and favors. It would be inconceivable without an ominous decline of individual independence and self-reliance, and above all, the burning desire to be free from man's bondage and to be responsible to God alone.

Can it happen again? Inexorable economic law ascertains that it must happen again whenever we repeat the dreadful errors that generated the Great Depression.

Entrepreneurs and the State

by Burton W. Folsom, Jr.

The big story in the U.S. auto industry during 1987 was the sharp growth (+35 percent) in sales for Honda and the decline (-3 percent) for Chrysler. While Honda sold cars as fast as it could make them, Chrysler struggled with a huge backlog of 1987 models. These results should not surprise us—they are part of a long historical pattern: federally aided companies, like Chrysler with its federally guaranteed loans, rarely outperform those that have to succeed on their own merits.

Those risk-takers who have sought and received help from the state we will call political entrepreneurs; those who have succeeded without it we will call market entrepreneurs. In steamships and railroads, two of the largest industries in the U.S. during the 1800s, these two groups of entrepreneurs regularly clashed, just as they do today.

Almost from the time of the first trans-Atlantic voyage by steam in the 1830s, the governments of England and the United States subsidized steamship travel. Samuel Cunard, a political entrepreneur, convinced the English government to give him $275,000 a year to run a biweekly mail and passenger service across the Atlantic. Cunard charged $200 per passenger and 24 cents a letter, but still said that he needed the annual aid to cover his losses. He contended that subsidized steamships gave England an advantage in world trade and were a readily available merchant marine in case of war. Parliament accepted this argument and increased government aid to the Cunard Line throughout the 1840s.

Soon, Edward Collins, a political entrepreneur across the ocean, began using these same arguments for federal aid to the new U.S. steamship industry. He said that America needed subsidized steamships to compete with England, to create jobs, and to provide a military fleet in case of war. If the government would give him $3 million

---

Dr. Folsom is Professor of History at Murray State University in Kentucky. This article, which appeared in the April 1988 issue of *The Freeman,* was adapted from his book *The Myth of the Robber Barons.*

Cornelius Vanderbilt
(1794–1877)

down and $385,000 a year, he would build five ships, deliver mail and passengers, and outrace the Cunarders from coast to coast.

Congress gave this money to Collins in 1847, but he built four enormous ships (not five smaller ships as he had promised), each with elegant saloons, ladies' drawing rooms, and wedding berths. He covered the ships with plush carpet and brought aboard olive-wood furniture, marble tables, exotic mirrors, painted glass windows, and French chefs. Collins stressed luxury, not economy, and his ships used almost twice the coal of the Cunard Line. He often beat the Cunarders across the ocean by one day, but his costs were high and his economic benefits were nil.

With annual government aid, Collins had no incentive to reduce his costs from year to year. He preferred to compete in the world of politics for more federal aid than in the world of business against price-cutting rivals. In 1852 he went to Washington and lavishly entertained President Fillmore, his cabinet, and influential Congressmen. Collins artfully lobbied Congress for an increase to $858,000 a year.

It took Cornelius Vanderbilt, a New York shipping genius, to challenge this system. In 1855, Vanderbilt offered to deliver the mail for less than half of what Collins was getting. Congress balked—it was pledged to Collins—so Vanderbilt decided to challenge Collins even without a subsidy. "The share of prosperity which has fallen to my lot," said Vanderbilt, "is the direct result of unfettered trade, and unrestrained competition. It is my wish that those who are to come after me shall have the same field open before them."

Vanderbilt's strategy against Collins was to cut the standard first-class fare to $80. He also introduced a cheaper third-class fare in the steerage. The steerage must have been uncomfortable—people were practically stacked on top of each other—but for $75, and sometimes less, he did get newcomers to travel.

Vanderbilt also had little or no insurance on his fleet: he built his ships well, hired excellent captains, and saved money on repairs and insurance. Finally, Vanderbilt hired local "runners" who buttonholed all kinds of people to travel on his ships. These second- and third-class passengers were important because all steamship operators had fixed costs for each voyage. They had to pay a set amount for coal, crew, maintenance, food, and docking fees. In such a situation, Vanderbilt needed volume business and sometimes carried over 500 passengers per ship.

All this was too much for Collins. When he tried to counter with more speed, he crashed two of his four ships, killing almost 500 passengers. In desperation he spent $1,000,000 of government money building a gigantic replacement, but he built it so poorly that it could make only two trips and had to be sold at more than a $900,000 loss.

Finally, Congress was outraged. Senator Robert M. T. Hunter of Virginia said: "The whole system was wrong . . . it ought to have been left, like any other trade, to competition." Senator John B. Thompson of Kentucky concurred: "Give neither this line, nor any other line, a subsidy. . . . Let the Collins Line die. . . . I want a tabula rasa—the whole thing wiped out, and a new beginning." Congress voted for this "new beginning" in 1858: they revoked Collins' aid and left him to compete with Vanderbilt on an equal basis. The results: Collins quickly went bankrupt, and Vanderbilt became the leading American steamship operator.

And there was yet another twist. When Vanderbilt competed against the English, his major competition did not come from the Cunarders. The new unsubsidized William Inman Line was doing to Cunard in England what Vanderbilt had done to Collins in America. The subsidized Cunard had cautiously stuck with traditional technology, while William Inman had gone on to use screw propellers and iron hulls instead of paddle wheels and wood. Inman's strategy worked; and from 1858 to the Civil War, two market entrepreneurs, Vanderbilt and Inman, led America and England in cheap mail and passenger service. The mail subsidies, then, ended up retarding progress: Cunard and Collins both used their monopolies to stifle innovation and delay technological changes in steamship construction.

Unfortunately, this cycle of government subsidy, mismanagement, and bankruptcy repeated itself a few years later in the railroad industry. With California and the Rocky Mountains safely in the Union, some people wanted a transcontinental railroad to tie the country together. Political entrepreneurs of the day convinced Congress that without federal aid the nation could not be linked by rail. Most historians have bought this argument, too. The late Thomas Bailey, whose textbook, *The American Pageant,* has sold over two million copies, said, "Transcontinental railroad building was so costly and risky as to require government subsidies." Congress adopted this logic and gave almost 100 million acres and $61 million in federal loans to four transcontinentals.

With massive federal aid came unprecedented corruption. The Union Pacific and Central Pacific built shoddy lines very quickly just to capture the federal subsidies. Also, the Credit Mobilier scandal, in which Union Pacific officials bribed Congressmen with cheap stock in return for favorable votes, rocked the Grant Administration and branded the whole railroad industry as corrupt. Eventually, negative public reaction helped lead to the establishment of the Interstate Commerce Commission. Congress, in effect, said that federal regulation was the solution to the problems created by federal aid.

Fortunately, James J. Hill, a market entrepreneur, showed the country how to build a different kind of transcontinental. From 1879 to 1893 he built the Great Northern Railroad from St. Paul to Seattle with no federal subsidy. Slowly, methodically, and with the best technology of his day he built a model line—relatively straight, on an even grade, and with high quality steel. He made each piece pay for itself before he moved further west. During the depression of the 1890s, when the subsidized Union Pacific, Northern Pacific, and Santa Fe Railroads went bankrupt, Hill ran his line profitably each year.

State aid—and this includes tariffs as well as loans—is always well intentioned. From Edward Collins to Lee Iacocca those who seek such aid really believe they have their nation's best interest at heart: they are protecting jobs, helping local industries compete, and preserving the industrial future of the nation. It is sad to see the opposite so often happen. Chrysler did pay back its loans—but it appears to be following the historical pattern set long ago in steamships and railroads.

The Postal Monopoly

by Brian Summers

In 1974 six children in New Jersey earned a few dollars by delivering Christmas cards for five cents each—half the United States Postal Service rate. They were breaking the law.[1]

In 1971 a private corporation, the Independent Postal System of America, offered to deliver Christmas cards for five cents each—three cents less than the U.S.P.S. rate. They were stopped by a court injunction.[2]

In 1966 the CF&I Steel Corporation, frustrated by the quality of postal service between their Denver headquarters and their plant in Pueblo, hired an armored-car service to deliver the mail. After five months of operation the service was halted by the Denver Post Office, and "at the Post Office's suggestion" CF&I paid $2,000 toward back postage.[3]

These are examples of a monopoly at work. With a few minor exceptions, the United States Postal Service enjoys a *legal* monopoly in the delivery of letters. Under the Private Express Statutes, private letter carriers are subject to fine and/or imprisonment.

Why should the U.S.P.S. hold a legal monopoly? And, more to the point, why should the government be carrying mail at all?

Let us examine some of the arguments put forward by defenders of the monopoly. One argument is that the U.S.P.S. constitutes a "natural" monopoly. That is, it is contended, it would be impossible for competing private firms to provide efficient service. Thus, it is argued, we need a government-run monopoly.

This argument does not stand up in the light of history. In the past three hundred years, thousands of private carriers have provided efficient postal service in England and America.

Three such private carriers stand out in British history: William Dockwra, Charles Povey, and Peter Williamson.[4] Each of these men was so efficient in providing postal service that the British General

---

Mr. Summers, former senior editor of *The Freeman,* is an editor with *Reader's Digest.* This article originally appeared in the March 1976 issue of *The Freeman.*

Post Office, after closing them down, adopted many of their methods.

William Dockwra established his London Penny Post in April 1680. Within a few months he had four hundred post offices, and was making ten daily deliveries and four to twelve daily collections. Thus, it was possible to send a letter and receive an answer the same day. The 1946 edition of the *Encyclopedia Britannica* reports:

> The staff employed in London by Dockwra considerably exceeded that employed by the post office in the whole kingdom. This truly remarkable enterprise gave London a postal service which in some respects has never been equalled before or since.
>
> For some time Dockwra struggled with serious financial difficulties; but no sooner had the penny post begun to show a profit than the duke of York, on whom the post office revenues were settled, asserted his monopoly. Dockwra was condemned to pay damages and his undertaking was incorporated in the General Post Office; but the London penny post long survived its creator and was maintained until 1801.

Charles Povey founded his Half-Penny Carriage in October 1709, serving parts of London, Westminster, and the borough of Southwark. His rates were less than the General Post Office. After seven months of operation he was fined and put out of business.

Peter Williamson established his Edinburgh Penny Post in 1776. He was so successful that his wife and father-in-law soon set up a competing penny post. After seventeen years his business was taken over by the General Post Office.

Following the lead of these three men, private penny posts sprung up all over the British Isles. According to one source, by 1800 there were over two thousand.[5] Today, due to the vigorous enforcement of the British postal monopoly, there are none.

The American story is much the same. In the nineteenth century hundreds of private carriers successfully competed with the Post Office Department. Due to the enforcement of the Private Express Statutes, none have survived.

One of the earliest of these postal services was begun in 1835 by William F. Harnden of Boston. His success encouraged competition, and by 1843 Boston alone had at least twenty private postal operators, including Alvin Adams, father of the Adams Express Company.

Soon private post offices dotted the land. There were Hussey's Post and Boyd's City Express in New York City; Pomeroy's Letter Express in eastern New York State; the Letter Express Company in western New York State, Chicago, and Detroit; Hale and Company in New York, New England, Philadelphia, and Baltimore; Lysander Spooner's American Letter Mail Company; Blood's New York Express (four deliveries and five collections daily); Wells and Company (later to become Wells Fargo); Yankee Jim's Loon Creek Express; Randall and Jones Canyon City Express—one stamp catalogue lists 150 private carriers. In 1845 private carriers transported an estimate one-third of the nation's letters.[6]

How efficient were the private carriers? *Hunt's Merchant Magazine* reported: "Government enterprise is wholly unable, under its most advantageous promptings, to compare with private enterprise."[7] Albert D. Richardson wrote that the Wells-Fargo Express operation in the West "illustrates the superiority of private enterprise. Whenever the messengers run on the very steamer, or the same railway carriage, with those of the United States mail, three-fourths of the businessmen entrust them with their letters, which are invariably delivered in advance of government consignments. . . ."[8]

Of course, these developments were noted in Washington. In 1844 Senator James F. Simmons of Rhode Island declared: "The fact is notorious that, . . . on the express routes, twenty letters are sent outside the mail for the one that is carried by the mail."[9] That same year Congressman John P. Hale of New Hampshire warned: "events are in progress of fatal tendency to the Post Office Department; and its decay has commenced."[10] The Philadelphia postmaster predicted that if the private carriers "be not put down, they will ere long put down the Post Office Department."[11]

Unable to match the efficiency of the private carriers, the Post Office resorted to force. The Private Express Statutes were strengthened in 1845. William C. Wooldridge reports:

> With a realistic appreciation of the underlying difficulties, the Senate Post Office Committee brought in a bill that would combine a drastic reduction in postage rates with stiffer restraints on private competition. Even then, however, the bill's sponsor recognized the government's congenital inability to compete successfully with the private expresses; he begged his

> colleagues "to keep in mind, what he had so repeatedly urged, that it was not by competition but by penal enactment" the private posts were to be destroyed.[12]

Those private carriers who weren't frightened from the market were put out of business by criminal prosecution. The government's postal monopoly was preserved, not by providing better service than the private carriers, but by threatening them with arrest.

There is nothing "natural" about the postal monopoly. If the monopoly were "natural," the government wouldn't have to crush competition with threats and criminal indictments.

A second argument used by the monopolists is that private carriers wouldn't charge uniform rates. They would charge less for low-cost routes (such as across town) than for high-cost routes (such as across the continent).

That sounds like a pretty fair system. People would pay for what they got. What we have now is across-town mailers being plundered to subsidize across-continent mailers. What is so noble about that?

And we should remember the words of *Hunt's Merchant Magazine:* "Government enterprise is wholly unable, under its most advantageous promptings, to compare with private enterprise." Given a few years of free enterprise, *all* postage rates would probably be lower than they are now, including those now subsidized by the taxpayers. Of course, we will never know as long the U.S.P.S. has a monopoly.

A third argument used by the monopolists is that private letters wouldn't be safe in the hands of private carriers. Private carriers might open the mail and read it.

This is precisely what the postal monopoly has been doing for years:

> For 20 years the CIA routinely opened over 13,000 letters a year going to and from the U.S.S.R., and later extended this operation to include mail from North Vietnam, Cuba, and other (noncommunist) Latin American countries. Chief Postal Inspector William Cotter systematically lied about the existence of this operation until just this year.
>
> Military counterintelligence groups routinely opened military mail, both within the U.S. and at overseas bases. The "flap and seal" operation was justified on the grounds of detecting

spies, but according to columnist Jack Anderson, was used largely to spy on servicemen who had complained about the Vietnam War.

In just the past two years, Inspector Cotter admits there have been 43 court orders for opening first class mail, and nearly 8600 approved mail covers [the recording of all return addresses on someone's incoming mail]. The latter have been at the behest of 41 Federal agencies, including the IRS, the Drug Enforcement Agency, the Interstate Commerce Commission and the Departments of Agriculture and Interior, as well as state and local police and prosecutors.[13]

On July 13, 1855, the editor of *Alta California,* enraged by the prosecution of private carriers declared: "The present Post Office system is the most outrageous tyranny ever imposed on a free people. It forbids us from sending letters by such means of conveyance as we may prefer, without paying an odious and onerous tax to the government."[14]

Strong words. And still true.

---

1. *The New York Times,* December 20, 1974 (New Jersey Edition).
2. John Haldi, *Postal Monopoly* (Washington, D. C.: American Enterprise Institute, 1974), pp. 16–17.
3. *The Wall Street Journal,* June 5, 1967.
4. Rockford Fresnel, "Postmen Against the State," *Innovator,* June 1966.
5. *Ibid.*
6. William C. Wooldridge, *Uncle Sam, The Monopoly Man* (New Rochelle, N.Y.: Arlington House, 1970), pp. 11–31.
7. Frank Chodorov, *The Myth of the Post Office* (Hinsdale, Ill.: Regnery, 1948), p. 14.
8. Wooldridge, p. 21.
9. George L. Priest, "The History of the Postal Monopoly in the United States," *Journal of Law & Economics,* April 1975, p. 59.
10. Priest, p. 61.
11. Wooldridge, p. 22.
12. Wooldridge, p. 23.
13. Robert Poole, Jr., "Getting Big Brother Out of the Mailbox," *Reason,* November 1975, p. 54.
14. Wooldridge, p. 31.

The Genesis of Industrial Policy

by Thomas J. DiLorenzo

Milton Friedman recently proposed the following syllogism which he believes characterizes much contemporary thinking about economic policy and institutions: Socialism has failed miserably wherever it has been attempted. The entire world knows this. Therefore, the world needs more socialism! This bizarre chain of "reasoning" is nowhere more prevalent than in contemporary proposals for a national industrial policy—governmental economic planning by a "tripartite" commission of politicians, businessmen, and union leaders.

So-called industrial policy was roundly criticized by nearly all mainstream economists—liberals and conservatives alike—during the early and mid-1980s. There is wide agreement that this "halfway house" between central planning and a free market economy, as Friedrich Hayek described it, is fundamentally flawed: Governmental planners cannot possibly possess the knowledge required for efficient resource allocation. Only the market and price system can efficiently distill the massive information required. The idea that a group of government planners can imitate market resource allocation is what Hayek calls "the fatal conceit."[1]

Moreover, in a democracy, governmental economic planning schemes are bound to be influenced more by political than by economic criteria. A national industrial policy would subsidize only politically powerful businesses, industries, and unions at the expense of diminishing overall economic growth.

Despite the avalanche of criticism, and the well-known failures of all socialistic economic planning schemes, the philosophical and ideological roots of industrial policy run deep. Like the character "Jason" in the *Friday the Thirteenth* horror films, the idea just never dies. Logic, reasoning, and evidence don't seem to faze its adherents. They persis-

---

Dr. DiLorenzo, a contributing editor of *The Freeman,* is Professor of Economics in the Sellinger School of Business Management at Loyola College in Baltimore. This article, which is adapted from his book *Paved With Good Intentions: Economic Nationalism and American Industrial Policy* (Cato Institute, 1990), appeared in the June 1990 issue of *The Freeman.*

tently relabel and repackage the same hoary notions, hoping they will catch on if only they are repeated often enough. Consider the recent history of the crusade for an interventionist industrial policy.

In the mid-1970s economist Wassily Leontief convened an "Initiative Committee for National Economic Planning" which, fortunately, never got off the ground. The phrase "national economic planning" was just too reminiscent of the spectacle of "planned" economies in Eastern Europe, the Soviet Union, and elsewhere, and the American public wanted no part of it.

The industrial policy proponents went right back to the drawing board and focused on a series of new marketing strategies. As Ira Magaziner, a strong proponent of industrial policy, candidly revealed: "Some of us started raising concerns about the decline of America's industrial base back in 1977; the solutions were labeled industrial policy, which became dirty words. Well, the problem didn't go away, so the concept re-emerged as 'industrial strategy.' Then we talked about 'competitiveness policies' and, most recently, 'industry-led strategies.' We've had four different names for what we should be doing without doing anything."[2]

What's in a Name?

There are other euphemisms for industrial policy, such as "economic democracy," "investment economics," and Michael Dukakis' "strategy for industrial America," which he tried to sell to the electorate in 1988.

More imaginative euphemisms for national economic planning are sure to be invented in the future. Magaziner and Harvard's Robert Reich, among others, have recently published new books promoting the same industrial policy potions they began peddling over a decade ago, and there is strong support for some kind of industrial policy in the business community and the union movement. Despite the wishes of free-market economists, this issue is not likely to fade any time soon.

Why the stubborn support for such a thoroughly discredited idea? One reason, I will argue, is that industrial policy proponents are largely oblivious to both economics and history. But if they had a better understanding of the doctrinal history of industrial policy, they might not be so enthusiastic about it. The origins of industrial policy are in an economic system that industrial policy proponents themselves would abhor—Fascism.

Contemporary proponents of industrial policy advocate many of the same *economic* policies that prevailed in Italy and Germany in the 1920s and '30s. They do *not* condone the abolition of civil and political liberties, the fanatical hero worship, the anti-Semitism, the violence, and the many other evils associated with Fascism. They are simply unaware that: (1) Fascism was an economic as well as a political and social debacle; and (2) Fascist economics was almost identical to so-called industrial policy.

Perilous Parallels

The "partnership" approach to national economic planning is one of the hallmarks of industrial policy. A 1989 United Automobile Workers publication outlines the familiar proposal for "development of a National Strategic Planning Board, made up of representatives of government, labor, businesses, and others to set goals for American industrial development, as well as specific committees on which labor, government, and business representatives would formulate plans for America's auto, steel, and other industries." This plan would supposedly "get labor, management, and government together to bargain a direction for our economy and specific industries."[3]

Business support for industrial policy is typified by a report by the Center for National Policy entitled "Rebuilding American Competitiveness." The report was written by academicians, government officials, and businessmen such as Felix Rohatyn of Lazard Freres & Co., former Du Pont Chairman Irving Shapiro, and representatives of the Chrysler and Burroughs corporations, among others. It calls for a "new approach to industrial policy" that is "based on *cooperation* of government with business and labor [emphasis in original]." Such cooperation would be institutionalized by "an Industrial Development Board, composed of government, labor, and business leaders" who would "develop cooperative strategies to promote industrial growth."[4]

Then of course there are the intellectual supporters of industrial policy, such as Robert Reich, Robert Solow, Lester Thurow, and Bennett Harrison of M.I.T., Barry Bluestone of Boston University, and various others. These individuals are among a number of academicians associated with a Washington, D.C.-based organization called "Rebuild America" which advocates "public-private partnerships among government, business and academia."[5]

But the idea of government/business partnerships is anything but new. It was in fact the heart of German and Italian economic policy during the 1920s and '30s. As the Italian Fascist Fausto Pitigliani wrote in 1934, Italian Fascism grouped businesses and unions into "legally recognized syndicates," the purpose of which was "to secure collaboration between the various categories of producers [i.e., employers and workers] in each particular trade. . . ."

The vehicle through which government, business, and unions would "coordinate" their plans was a network of government economic planning agencies, which the Italian Fascists called "corporations." The corporations were organized industry-wide and were intended to "secure permanent collaboration between employers and workers." These corporations were Mussolini's version of the tripartite commissions that contemporary industrial policy proponents advocate.

In Fascist Italy there was one National Council, which Fascist author Gaetano Salvemini claimed was established "to exercise very considerable influence upon the development of the means of production in the national economic life of Italy."[6] Another Fascist apologist, Luigi Villari, wrote in 1932 that such business/government partnerships promoted "a spirit of national collaboration which would not be possible under any other system."[7] The Italian National Council sounds nearly identical to the U.A.W.'s "National Strategic Planning Boards."

The National Socialist (Nazi) government in Germany established its own economic-planning scheme that was very similar to the Italian system (and to contemporary industrial policy proposals). As described by historian Franz Neuman, there was a "National Economic Chamber," the duty of which was "to co-ordinate the territorial and the functional setup" of industry. This National Economic Chamber was a federal overseer of numerous local chambers, similar to the Italian Fascist system.

In a statement that could have been written by one of the contemporary American proponents of industrial policy, the German newspaper *Deutsche Volkswirt* explained in 1933 that the purpose of these institutions was to "give private industry possibilities and tasks for far-reaching collaboration."[8] According to the Nazi National Economic Minister, "Our task is the limited one of coordinating with the present idea of national government the organization of the enormous field of German business administration."[9] As in the industrial policy literature, the words "cooperation" and "collaboration" were used repeatedly by German and Italian Fascists.

The "Unity of Aim" Argument

One of the most persistent arguments made by proponents of a national industrial policy goes something like this: We've already got industrial policies—regulation, direct subsidies, protectionism, credit subsidies, selective tax breaks for certain industries—but they are too *ad hoc,* overlapping, piecemeal, and sometimes contradictory. What's needed is a more centralized or national industrial plan with clearly defined and fixed objectives.

As Lester Thurow has written: "We already have industrial policies. . . . The only real question is whether America has effective front-door industrial policies in which we consciously attempt to design a strategy to give America a viable world class economy or whether we fail to recognize what we are doing and have back-door industrial policies with a case-by-case adoption."[10]

Former Carter domestic policy adviser Stuart Eizenstat claimed that a national industrial policy would "be a more effective organization of what every President since George Washington has been doing in a piecemeal, uncoordinated way."[11] And the Center for National Policy claims that "to argue that government should not have industrial policies is to ignore the fact that it does." What is lacking, says the Center, "are efforts to coordinate . . . all these different policies."[12] Similar statements are repeated over and over again in the industrial policy literature.

Again, such thinking is nearly identical to what was being said in Italy and Germany in the 1920s and '30s. Mussolini himself stated in 1934 that existing government intervention into the Italian economy was "too diverse, varied, contrasting. There has been disorganic intervention, case by case, as the need arises." Fascism would supposedly "remedy" this, wrote Mussolini, because it promised to "introduce order in the economic field" and direct the economy toward "certain fixed objectives."[13]

The whole purpose of the Italian economic planning apparatus, according to Pitigliani, was to give industry "unity of aim" and to "bring together under a single administration the productive forces of the nation."[14] Admiration for central planning, in other words, is one thing the industrial policy proponents have in common with early twentieth-century Fascists.

The Inherent Failures of Industrial Policy

The essence of early twentieth-century German and Italian industrial policy (and of contemporary industrial policy proposals) was for government, business, and unions to attempt to "collaborate to coordinate" the economy in the public interest. Individual consumers, businesses, investors, and workers supposedly couldn't be relied upon to serve national rather than individual interests. "The function of private enterprise," wrote Pitigliani, "is assessed from the standpoint of public interest, and hence an owner or director of a business undertaking is responsible before the State for his production policy."[15] Fifty years later, the Center for National Policy similarly advocated an "Industrial Development Board" that would "identify sectors of the economy crucial to the national interest" and provide "public [i.e., taxpayer] support as part of an overall development strategy."[16] The theme of economic nationalism pervades both the industrial policy literature and the literature of Fascism.

Despite the public-interest rhetoric, business/government collaboration in Germany and Italy constituted a mammoth conspiracy against the public. Business and government collaborated to milk the taxpayers for subsidies to big business and to establish a vast system of government sanctioned cartels. As a disenchanted Gaetano Salvemini wrote in 1936, although the Fascist "Charter of Labor says that private enterprise is responsible to the state . . . it is the state, i.e., the taxpayer, who has become responsible to private enterprise. In Fascist Italy the state pays for the blunders of private enterprise."

As long as business was good, wrote Salvemini, "profit remained to private initiative." Loss, however, "is public and social." Mussolini boasted in 1934 that "three-quarters of the Italian economic system, both industrial and agricultural, had been subsidized by government."[17] By subsidizing business failure on such a grand scale, Italian Fascism guaranteed a failing economy.

Such business/government collaboration also created a system of monopolies through massive regulation that could forbid the creation of new factories or the development of existing plants. As reported in *The Economist* on July 27, 1935, the Italian "Corporative State only amounts to the establishment of a new and costly bureaucracy from which those industrialists who can spend the necessary amount, can obtain almost anything they want, and put into practice the worst kind of monopolistic practices. . . ."[18]

There was also a "revolving door" between government and industry—the familiar practice of government bureaucrats dishing out subsidies to industry, and then retiring from government to take well-paying jobs in the industries they had previously been "regulating."

German industrial policy also glorified the notion of business/government collaboration, but it too was nothing but the most ordinary protectionism. Regulations prohibited price-cutting and established a system of government-sponsored monopolies, described by Hayek as "a sort of syndicalist or 'corporative' organization of industry, in which competition is more or less suppressed but planning is left in the hands of the independent monopolies of the separate industries."[19] Government/business collaboration, admitted a Nazi economist, "gives a cartel a power which it could not obtain on a voluntary basis."[20]

Lessons of History

One doesn't need to go as far back in history as Mussolini's Italy or Nazi Germany to observe how collaboration between government, business, and unions breeds corruption and monopolization. The recent HUD and savings and loan scandals are typical examples of the inherent failures of government/industry collaboration. In each instance, businesses and government officials collaborated to benefit personally at great expense to the general taxpaying public.

In 1978 the Carter Administration implemented a textbook example of the partnership approach to industrial policy. It "cooperated" with the United Steelworkers union and several steel companies to grant $265 million in loan guarantees to the companies through the federal government's Economic Development Administration (EDA). The objective was supposedly to save 50,000 jobs in four companies. By 1987 all four loans had defaulted, two of the companies had gone bankrupt, and the two others had filed for bankruptcy. The taxpayers were out $265 million and not a single job was "saved" in the steel industry.

As of April 1989, 55 percent of the EDA's loan portfolio was delinquent, with hundreds of millions of dollars in bad loans. The EDA's own staff admitted that its loan programs "would have to be considered a failure" and are "an excellent example of the folly inherent in industrial policy programs."[21]

Trucking regulation by the Interstate Commerce Commission, which cartelized the trucking industry, is another example of what one can expect from an interventionist industrial policy. Trucking firms, the Teamsters, and government collaborated to construct barriers to entry in the trucking business at great expense to consumers and potential competitors. Airline regulation by the Civil Aeronautics Board was another example of an industrial policy cartel.

Protectionism is an example of business/union/government collaboration for the purpose of organizing a price-fixing conspiracy against the public. As Adam Smith wrote in *The Wealth of Nations,* businessmen seldom meet, even for fun and entertainment, when the conversation does not turn to some kind of conspiracy against the public.

Private cartels are notoriously unstable. Consequently, monopolists have always favored "cooperation" between business, government, and unions: Only the coercive powers of the state can guarantee the survival of a privately organized cartel. Thus, monopoly is all too often the result of government/industry partnerships.

As the historical record of interventionist industrial policies becomes clearer, I predict the following syllogism will describe the attitudes of industrial-policy proponents: interventionist industrial policies have bred monopoly, corruption, and economic stagnation wherever they have been tried. Everyone knows this. Therefore, we need more industrial policy! Santayana's dictum, "Those who cannot remember the past are condemned to repeat it," is particularly relevant to the ongoing industrial-policy debate.

---

1. Friedrich Hayek, *The Fatal Conceit* (Chicago: University of Chicago Press, 1988).

2. "Why Managers Need a Little Help from Washington," *Business Month,* July 1989, p. 77.

3. "A UAW Action Agenda," U.A.W. Public Relations Department.

4. *Restoring American Competitiveness* (Washington, D.C.: Center for National Policy, 1984), pp. 7, 8.

5. *An Investment Economics for the Year 2000,* p. 32.

6. Fausto Pitigliani, *The Italian Corporative State* (New York: Macmillan, 1934), pp. 93, 98, 108.

7. Luigi Villari, "The Economics of Fascism," in his book, *Bolshevism, Fascism, and Capitalism* (New Haven: Yale University Press, 1932), p. 107.

8. Franz Neuman, *Behemoth: The Structure and Practice of National Socialism* (New York: Octagon Books, 1963), pp. 241, 359.

9. Cited in Robert A. Brady, *The Spirit and Structure of German Fascism* (New York: Howard Fertig, 1969), p. 105.

10. Lester Thurow, "The Case for Industrial Policies," Center for National Policy, January 1984, p. 7.

11. Stuart Eizenstat, "Industrial Policy: Not If, But How," *Fortune,* January 23, 1984, p. 183.

12. *Restoring American Competitiveness,* p. 10.

13. Benito Mussolini, *Fascism: Doctrine and Institutions* (Rome: Adrita Press, 1935), p. 68; reprinted in New York by Howard Fertig, Inc., 1968.

14. Pitigliani, p. 117.

15. *Ibid.,* p. x.

16. *Restoring American Competitiveness,* p. *13.*

17. Gaetano Salvemini, *Under the Axe of Fascism* (New York: King Press, 1936), p. 380.

18. *The Economist* (editorial), July 27, 1935.

19. Friedrich Hayek, *The Road to Serfdom* (Chicago: University of Chicago Press, 1944), p. 41.

20. Cited in Neuman, p. 268.

21. Warren Brookes, "The Big Steel That Never Made It," *Washington Times,* April 10, 1989.

IV. OVERCOMING THE OBSTACLES

The Little Railroad That Could

by Anthony Young

Woven into the rich fabric of American history and folklore are some of the most famous railroads still operating today. You needn't be a railroad buff to recognize them: the Atchison, Topeka and Santa Fe (established 1895), the Grand Trunk Western (1852), and the Union Pacific (1862) to name just three. Among these great railroads are those created recently by mergers of existing companies, with names like Conrail, Burlington Northern, and CSX. Of the thirteen Class I freight carriers operating in the United States, the smallest is the Florida East Coast Railway (FEC).[1]

The FEC operates only 783 miles of track between its Jacksonville headquarters and Miami, but in a heavily regulated and unionized industry, it is a model of efficiency and profitability. How has this small railroad, established in 1895, managed to survive and prosper in an industry that has seen countless railroads, both great and small, vanish from the scene?

The Flagler System

Railroading has always attracted the thickest-skinned entrepreneurs—captains of industry and empire builders. This was true of even a small railroad like the FEC. Henry Morrison Flagler (1830–1913) was such a man. The partnership he formed with John D. and William Rockefeller to operate a small refinery in Cleveland eventually grew to become the Standard Oil Company of Ohio. He became a multimillionaire, and by the 1880s was looking for new empires to build.

In the winter of 1883–84 he visited St. Augustine, Florida. He thought the small city charming and the climate to his liking, but found the accommodations lacking. While considering building a luxury hotel, he became convinced that he could make St. Augustine a travel destination for wealthy Americans. He announced plans to build a hotel to rival anything in Europe, and that was to be the draw.

This article was published in the May 1992 issue of *The Freeman*.

COURTESY NEW-YORK HISTORICAL SOCIETY

Henry Morrison Flagler
(1830–1913)

To get the vast quantities of construction material to the burgeoning city and offer a route to his new hotel, Flagler purchased the bonds to the Jacksonville, St. Augustine and Halifax River Railway. The Ponce de Leon opened in January 1888, the first of many luxury hotels Flagler would build or refurbish in Florida. These became known as the Flagler System Hotels.

Flagler realized that the means of expanding Florida tourism was the railroad, and he began acquiring other lines along the state's east coast. In 1888 the first all-Pullman vestibule train began running between New York and Florida. He built a bridge across the St. Johns River to permit trains to travel directly to St. Augustine; before, passengers traveled to Jacksonville and took a ferry across the river, then traveled by train to St. Augustine.

Pushing farther south, Flagler established resorts in Palm Beach and Miami. In the spring of 1892, he incorporated a new line, the Florida Coast and Gulf Railway. Later that year, he changed the name to the Jacksonville, St. Augustine and Indian River Railway. In 1895 this became the Florida East Coast Railway, and Flagler merged his other railroads under this banner.

With vision some called folly, Flagler set his sights on Key West as the railroad's final destination. This massive engineering project, called the Key West Extension, was begun in 1904 and completed in 1912 at a cost of tens of millions of dollars and a loss of more than 700 lives due to storms, diseases, and other mishaps. On the inaugural trip from New York to Key West, Flagler rode in his private railway car, "Rambler." Nearly blind, he lived to witness, but not see, his greatest accomplishment. The "railroad that went to sea," as some called it, operated for 23 years, until it was destroyed by a hurricane in 1935.[2]

Both freight and passengers were vitally important to the FEC during the 1920s and 1930s. The Atlantic Coast Line Railway and the Seaboard Air Line Railroad were its chief competitors in Florida during this time and in the decades that followed. Forced to file for bankruptcy in the Great Depression year of 1931, the FEC continued to operate in receivership, yet stubbornly refused to go under.

Union Trouble

The FEC's most vexing problems ultimately would come from within, as well as from the government. Between 1950 and 1962, it earned a profit in only one year, 1955. The railroad lost over $29 million during that time.[3] In 1961 the Interstate Commerce Commission awarded trusteeship to Edward Ball, chairman of the board of the FEC, which was now a subsidiary of St. Joe Paper Company, itself a subsidiary of the Alfred I. duPont estate. As a trustee of the estate, Ball had been buying up the second mortgage bonds of the FEC since 1941. For the next 20 years, he was the railroad's greatest champion and defender. That did not include, however, supporting a bloated payroll. As part of reorganization efforts, he cut the number of employees from 3,300 to 2,200.

Ball conferred closely with two other officers of the company, Raymond W. Wyckoff and Winfred L. Thornton. They soon agreed that to save the railroad, they would have to challenge the unions. In 1962 the FEC refused union wage demands and decided to negotiate directly with its employees. One of the longest and most destructive strikes in American railroad history, involving five operating unions and 22 nonoperating unions (those not running the trains), began on January 23, 1963.

In the first 10 days of the strike, nothing moved on FEC tracks. Ed Ball was resolute: he would not acquiesce to union demands, despite intense pressure from the Kennedy Administration. Company officers made a bold decision. They would operate the railroad with supervisory personnel and employ new workers. The alternative was a return to bankruptcy. On February 3, 1963, the first train with a supervisory crew set out from the Bowden terminal in Jacksonville.

In the months that followed, hundreds of acts of violence and sabotage were committed against the railroad. These included removing rails, damaging switches, and firing gunshots at the locomotive cabs. There were several wrecks and in two instances trains were blown up, but there were no serious injuries or deaths.

No passengers were carried during the strike until the Florida Railroad and Public Utilities Commission (FR&PUC) examined the company's charter and ordered the FEC to reinstate passenger service. On August 2, 1965, passenger trains once again were running between Jacksonville and Miami, but the railroad warned passengers they traveled at their own risk.

Rail travel in general had been declining since the 1950s. The FEC had been losing money for years on its passenger service, and the strike exacerbated the situation. The company petitioned the FR&PUC to end service, and this was granted. The last FEC passenger train ran on July 31, 1968.

The strikes dragged on into the 1970s. Many railroad workers gave up hope of there ever being a settlement and moved on to other jobs, never to return to the industry. The strike by the non-operating unions didn't end until December 1974. The National Mediation Board finally called a halt to the strikes by the operating unions on May 3, 1977.

Cutting the Fat

The strike and subsequent operation by supervisory personnel and new hires proved to the FEC just how much featherbedding there had been. The railroad found it could operate with far fewer workers.

The FEC implemented changes that were radical for the industry—changes that would make the railroad profitable. The following work rules were eliminated:

1. The archaic 100-mile-day rule that required three separate five-man crews to move a train from Jacksonville to Miami. The FEC implemented an eight-hour day, plus time-and-a-half for overtime. In the process, they reduced the crew to two operators per train for the entire trip, eliminating 13 non-essential workers.

2. Restrictions on road crews operating within a terminal.

3. Rules preventing yard crews from performing road work, or vice versa.

4. Restrictions fixing the number of men in a yard or train crew.

5. Rules dictating when yard engines (locomotives) could be started.

The FEC also established a single seniority date—the date of hire—for all engine and train employees in both yard and road service, so that an employee could apply for the different positions he was qualified to hold without penalty. This has given employees unprecedented flexibility in planning their careers.

In addition, the FEC started an aggressive capital improvement program that today is the model for the industry. In the mid-1960s, the FEC began developing concrete ties, which are now used on all the company's main track from Jacksonville to Miami. This greatly reduces track maintenance and costs.

To insure safety and optimal equipment operation, automatic devices installed every 20 miles of track check for loose wheels, overheated journals, and dragging equipment, and verify the presence of the tail-end monitor since cabooses are no longer used. Overhead gantries fitted with photo-beams check for shifted loads every 40 miles.

The FEC's outstanding profits come from its ability to quickly load trailers coming off the interstate, usually two to a flatcar; keeping the trains short, usually 20 cars per train, permits quick turnaround and frequent departures held to a strict timetable. This piggyback service saves wear and tear on customer equipment, reduces driver fatigue, and cuts freight costs to and from Miami. High volume permits the FEC to keep its rates low.

A Lesson to Follow

Can the FEC's innovations be adopted by other railroads? This has been bandied about for years. Some railroads have adopted aspects of the FEC's operations, but these are exceptions. Others have tried, only to be driven back by the unions. Some industry analysts say the FEC's position is unique. Nevertheless, company officers would be the first to say procedures such as theirs *could* be implemented, but the industry mind-set precludes it. FEC president W. L. Thornton made his views clear: "The Florida East Coast has demonstrated how much you can do if you allow yourself not to be constrained by the way things *have* been done. You see all kinds of things done unconventionally on the FEC, at all levels—in the mechanical department, in operations, in the yards. One reason for this is that they brought in 'inexperienced' people instead of embracing the institutionalized verities that were there before them. Conventional wisdom went out the window, where it so often belongs."[4]

Clearly, the FEC's key executives have embraced this view for the past three decades. It would take a similar commitment for other, larger railroads to make comparable changes. In any event, the Florida East Coast Railway will continue to be an innovative leader, an example of what can be done if the will to do so is there.

---

1. The Interstate Commerce Commission ranks railroads according to size. Rail systems with operating revenues of $93.5 million or more are categorized Class 1.

2. Pat Parks, *The Railroad That Died at Sea* (Key West, Fla.: Langley Press, 1968), p. 38.

3. Seth H. Bramson, *Speedway to Sunshine* (Erin, Ontario, Canada: Boston Mills Press, 1984), p. 141.

4. Quoted by Luther S. Miller, editor, *Railway Age,* May 8, 1978.

Lessons from an Entrepreneur

by David N. Laband

The praise recently showered upon the late Sam Walton suggests that now is an opportune time to question the consistency with which Americans treat successful businessmen and to reaffirm the *universal* applicability of capitalism's Invisible Hand as a "mechanism" to promote consumer welfare.

On March 17, 1992, Sam Walton received the Presidential Medal of Freedom, the nation's highest civilian honor, from President George Bush. Upon Walton's death, the President remembered him as "an American original who embodied the entrepreneurial spirit and epitomized the American dream." Mr. Walton was not lionized by President Bush merely because of his entrepreneurial spirit; millions of Americans have entrepreneurial spirit. What made Sam Walton unique was his spectacular success as an entrepreneurial capitalist. Mr. Walton and his four children have become fabulously wealthy from their creation of over 1,735 Wal-Mart stores and 212 Sam's Wholesale Club warehouses throughout America. They ranked numbers three through seven on the most recent *Forbes* list of wealthiest Americans.

Sam Walton was an enormously successful free-market capitalist. An appropriate eulogy for him would include thanks for an economic system that rewards individuals who cater to consumers' wishes. The millions of Americans who have patronized his stores and contributed thereby to his immense wealth would do well to consider the meaning of Sam Walton's success story in terms of international trade.

Our admiration for Sam Walton goes far beyond mere awe of his fortune. Indeed, his great wealth reflects something far more significant. The cavils of anti-free-market fanatics notwithstanding, American consumers *voluntarily* made Sam Walton rich. The same individuals who seek to raise taxes on the rich because of their enviable position in the current income distribution probably buy merchandise at both

---

Professor Laband teaches in the Department of Economics and Finance, The Perdue School of Business, Salisbury State University, Salisbury, Maryland. This article originally appeared in the September 1992 issue of *The Freeman*.

Sam Walton

Wal-Mart and Sam's. They, like many other rational consumers, flock to Wal-Mart stores because of the low prices, the service, and the quality. In short, Sam Walton figuratively built a better mousetrap than his competitors, and with their many billions of dollar-votes American consumers demonstrated that they preferred his product. Those who continued to patronize *other* department stores and shops benefited too, as these stores were forced to lower their prices and improve their product lines and services to remain competitive. The personal wealth amassed by the Walton family pales in comparison to the cumulative benefits Sam Walton generated for virtually all American consumers.

However, in the process of making Sam Walton rich, American consumers impoverished many of Mr. Walton's competitors. Every dollar spent at Wal-Mart was a figurative dollar and a quarter not spent for similar merchandise at Sears, K-Mart, J. C. Penney, or any of the other large chain department stores. Perhaps more importantly, it was a dollar and fifty cents not spent at local, small businesses. Some owners of small businesses, unable to take advantage of Wal-Mart's huge economies of scale, sought to prevent Wal-Marts from being built in their local communities. The everyday low-price strategy employed by Wal-Mart would put them out of business, they argued. They were (and continue to be) half-correct. It is true that Wal-Mart's competitors lost business. However, let's get the cause and the effect straight: Wal-Mart never put anybody out of business, *American consumers* did.

Businesses that lose their competitive edge to a more efficient rival have three options. They can: (1) change their product/service mix to reflect more accurately what they do best, (2) exit the market, or (3) petition consumers and/or the state for protection against "unfair competition." The first two responses enhance consumer welfare. To the extent consumers *voluntarily* purchase more expensive, lower-quality goods produced by domestic manufacturers, no self-respecting economist would argue with their choices: *de gustibus non est disputandum.* However, the instant the state regulates to protect domestic firms from "unfair competition," the result is higher prices, reduced choice, and lower quality and service for American consumers.

Shooting the Messenger

Every effort by small businessmen to forestall the building of a Wal-Mart is an attempt to shoot the messenger rather than pay heed to the message. Local economies do not go to pot when Wal-Marts are built. Quite the opposite: Sam Walton once said, "There was a lot more business in those towns than people ever thought."

Without question, each Wal-Mart and Sam's store alters the structure of local unemployment. The sons and daughters of local businessmen and women no longer follow in their parents' proprietary footsteps. Now they, as well as many other local workers, go to work for Uncle Sam (Walton). Thus, the overall rate of local employment is generally not adversely affected. While we may feel sorry for the personal losses suffered by the owners of these no-longer competitive small firms, the aggregate benefits reaped by (all-too-often- forgotten) consumers, including those same small businessmen, outweigh their losses. If this were not true, Sam Walton would never have received the Presidential Medal of Freedom.

The pleas to local zoning boards and planning commissions for protection from "unfair competition" by small businesses faced with the prospect of having to compete with a new Wal-Mart store sound identical to the rhetoric employed by mouthpieces for the Big Three automobile companies, the textile and steel industries, sugar producers, and every other domestic industry seeking to restrict foreign sales of these products in America. To kick Japanese and other foreign producers out of American markets is to deny the benefits of Sam Walton-esque competition.

The negative impact of one business on another in the process of ordinary competition (price, service, quality, product line) is known among academic economists as a "technological externality." Technological externalities are the fingers of Adam Smith's Invisible Hand that guide producers to supply what consumers want, when they want it, at prices equal to cost of production. Any interference with these technological externalities, especially government interference, jeopardizes consumer welfare.

By invoking the rhetoric of "unfair competition," domestic firms seek deliberately to mislead consumers into thinking that protection of competitors is the same thing as protection of competition. Nothing could be further from the truth. Protection of the existing firms in an industry against more efficient competitors, be they American or foreign, insulates those firms from the forces of competition. American consumers are the worse for it: they pay higher prices for shoddier products than would be available in a more competitive environment.

Japan-bashing is equivalent to Sam Walton-bashing. The principles of competition are universal, whether the competitors are domestic or foreign. The fact that sellers are foreign does not diminish the potential gains to American consumers from competition between sellers. If we're going to lionize Sam Walton, consistency demands that we lionize *every* successful producer in the global economy.

Economic Prediction and Entrepreneurial Success

by Dennis L. Peterson

While traveling in my car recently, I was intrigued by an illustration given on an audio-cassette presentation to which I was listening. It set me to reflecting on the power of the human spirit in a free environment and the futility of government attempts to regulate and predict that spirit.

The speaker was Thomas J. Peters, author of the best-selling *In Search of Excellence.* In the process of discussing his thesis, Peters described a man who defied all the negative predictions and forecasts of the "experts" and created a $1.3 billion company. According to the "experts," what he did was impossible, and he did it in an area that would qualify for the "Least Likely to Succeed" award.

In every single year since 1930, the "experts" predicted that American consumers had had it with chicken. There was just no more demand for it on the market. Despite the same gloomy prediction for so many years, Frank Perdue "made it" with chicken! And he did it in the economically "depressed" Delmarva Peninsula. From that unlikely spot, he has successfully expanded into the largest urban areas of the eastern United States, including New York, Boston, Baltimore, Washington, D.C., and Philadelphia. His lowest share of any of these market areas is 50 percent.

The accomplishments of Frank Perdue and other entrepreneurs like him could not be predicted by government economists. Their successes are due to the imagination, creativity, and purposeful actions of free individuals in the free enterprise marketplace. They were spurred to these entrepreneurial heights by the desire to make a profit and thereby improve their lot in life. In the process, they met the needs of millions of similar individuals. None of this could have been accomplished by the mere manufacture of charts, graphs, and "guesstimates" by government's economic "experts."

Mr. Peterson is a frequent contributor to *The Freeman, Teaching Home,* and other periodicals. This article is adapted and updated from *The Freeman,* September 1985.

Frank Perdue

Charts and Statistics

One of the fallacies promulgated and perpetuated in many high school and college economics courses today is the idea that economics *is* charts, graphs, statistics, and predictions. Economics, when taught in such a manner, is perceived as a complex and mysterious realm into which only the "experts" dare venture. All the rest of us, then, are expected to act and react according to the predictions, presuppositions, and economic philosophies of these "experts."

"The only function of economic forecasting," Ezra Solomon stated, "is to make astrology look respectable." Another wag declared that if all the economic experts who ever lived were stretched out head-to-toe around the earth, they would never reach an accurate conclusion.

While charts, graphs, and statistics are appropriate for the study of *past* economic events, activities, or trends, they have little to do with predicting the quantitative actions of individuals in a free market. According to author and lecturer Earl Nightingale, the impression that "figures give you all the answers is wrong. Figures don't give you the answers. Figures merely give you the questions."

No less an authority than Ludwig von Mises showed the futility of government planning and prediction in the economy. "The most that can be attained with regard to reality is probability," he stated. "The fundamental economic problem," he continued, "consists in the neglect of the fact that there are no constant relations between what are called economic dimensions."

Statistics can also be distorted to fit the views and purposes of whoever is using them. As one of my college economics professors once said, "Figures don't lie, but sometimes liars do the figures!"

There are those who will argue, however, that whereas it may be true that government forecasting and planning were not necessary in the early stages of our nation's economic development, today's rapidly changing and highly technical industrial society make it essential. Joseph P. Kennedy firmly believed this. "An organized functioning society," he contended, "requires a planned economy. The more complex the society, the greater the demand for planning."

Once government officials adopt this fallacy as public policy, there is no end to the extremes of regulation and experimentation that government will undertake. It is this interference in the free market, more than any other single factor, which brings about inflation, unemployment, scarcity, and depression. And, ironically, these problems then lead to increased demands for government intervention.

John Chamberlain addressed so succinctly the problem created by such government interference in the market: "Where government tries to substitute itself for the economic motor, there is the inevitable confusion between the starter, the accelerator, and the brake."

"Fellows with Schemes"

Reduced to its simplest form, government interference through planning is the attempt by a few to tell the rest what is best for them, as though the individual is too ignorant to determine his own self-interests. Humorist Will Rogers might have had this in mind when he commented, "World ain't going to be saved by nobody's scheme. It's fellows with schemes that got us into this mess."

Psalm 127:1

Socialistic planners think in terms of a nebulous nonentity called "society." They think "society" produces goods and services. They think "society" consumes the goods and services "society" produces.

In reality, only individuals produce and consume. There is no economic action of the masses but only of individuals. Government actions in a free economy, therefore, must be based on this foundation principle. This precludes all government planning and interference in the economy beyond the requirements of defense and general safety.

After thinking about the phenomenal successes of Frank Perdue and other entrepreneurs like him, I wondered where we would be today had these entrepreneurs permitted government predictions to cloud their visions. Literally millions of consumers would have had needs unmet. Billions of dollars in economic activity would have been redirected into other channels. Many profitable jobs would never have come into existence. The experts' predictions would have been "proven" by self-fulfilling prophecy. The myth of economics as the realm of the experts would have been further perpetuated.

But these and other believers in the free market refused to be kept down by the gloom and doom forecasts of the planners. They knew that if they worked hard to meet the needs of consumers, produced quality products, and served their customers courteously, they would have a fantastically profitable market at their fingertips. They put their knowledge and imaginations to work and, with faith in the free-market system, made their dreams realities.

The attempts of such individuals—both their successes and their failures—are what the free market is all about. And it will continue to survive and thrive in spite of government interference. It operates best, however, when it is permitted total freedom.

Index

About The Foundation for Economic Education

The Foundation for Economic Education (FEE) is a "home" for the friends of freedom everywhere. Its spirit is uplifting, reassuring, contagious: FEE has inspired the creation of numerous similar organizations at home and abroad.

FEE is the oldest conservative research organization dedicated to the presentation of individual freedom and the private-property order. It was established in 1946 by Leonard E. Read, and guided by its adviser, the eminent Austrian economist, Ludwig von Mises. Both served FEE until their deaths in 1983 and 1973, respectively.

Throughout the years the mission of FEE has remained unchanged: to study the moral and intellectual foundation of a free society and share its knowledge with individuals everywhere. It avoids getting embroiled in heated political controversies raging in Washington, D.C. Located in Irvington-on-Hudson, New York, FEE has remained a purely educational organization.

Since 1956, FEE has published *The Freeman,* an award-winning monthly journal with a long and noble lineage. Under the profound editorship of Paul Poirot it rose to great heights, always fighting for the timeless principles of the free society.

The *Freeman Classics* series of books reflects these heights, consisting of topical collections of great essays and articles published throughout the years. *The Spirit of Freedom* is the tenth volume in the series. Also available: *The Morality of Capitalism, Private Property and Political Control, Prices and Price Controls, Public Education and Indoctrination, Politicized Medicine, Man and Nature, Taxation and Confiscation, Bankers and Regulators,* and *American Unionism: Fallacies and Follies.*

—Hans F. Sennholz

PRICE LIST

The Spirit of Freedom

Quantity	Price Each
1 copy	$14.95
2-4 copies	12.00
5-49 copies	9.00
50-499 copies	7.50
500 copies	6.00